Creation
or
Evolution

Creation
or
Evolution

Correspondence
on the
Current Controversy

Edward O. Dodson
and
George F. Howe

University of Ottawa Press
Ottawa • London • Paris

© University of Ottawa Press, 1990
ISBN 0-7766-0313-2 (cloth)
ISBN 0-7766-0269-1 (paper)
Printed and bound in Canada

Canadian Cataloguing in Publication Data

Dodson, Edward O. (Edward Ottway), 1916–
Creation or evolution

ISBN 0-7766-0313-2 (bound)
ISBN 0-7766-0269-1 (pbk.)

1. Dodson, Edward O. (Edward Ottway), 1916–
— Correspondence. 2. Howe, George F. (George
Franklin), 1931–   — Correspondence.
3. Evolution — Religious aspects — Christianity —
Controversial literature. 4. Creationism —
Controversial literature. 5. Salvation —
Controversial literature.   I. Howe, George F.
(George Franklin), 1931– .   II. Title.

BS659.D64 1990   231.7′65   C90-090169-1

UNIVERSITÉ UNIVERSITY
D'OTTAWA   OF OTTAWA

Design: Judith Gregory

Contents

Foreword

The Controversy

uestions on the origin of life and of the universe must have challenged primeval human curiosity and imagination as soon as early man acquired time for activities not directly associated with survival. A yearning for explanations of mankind's origin, function, purpose, and ultimate destiny seems as innate to humans as the power of reason and a proclivity to believe in the supernatural. Philosophers, natural scientists, and theologians have dealt with these issues in various ways, depending on the assumptions of their respective disciplines and on the personal convictions they bring to their enquiries. Without questioning the integrity of the motives of those truth-seekers, one may still find it difficult, if not impossible, to distinguish between objective analyses of fact and subjective expressions of predisposition in their writings. A clear distinction between the natural and the supernatural is not always forthcoming. The omission of truths, particularly recently discovered ones, also contributes to the haze that hangs heavy over interdisciplinary discussions in these areas.

Along with the accelerating growth of knowledge through scientific discovery and the burgeoning of technological power, humanity now faces the overshadowing prospect of self-extinction. The challenge to survival raises urgent questions about values, ethical systems, human rights and freedoms, social governance, moral bases for civil law, and the purpose and destiny of mankind. What seemed in the past to be esoteric questions reserved for philosophers and theologians with their feet planted firmly in the clouds, or scientists hidden away in ivory tower laboratories, have now become urgent and even terrifying issues requiring immediate attention and prompt resolution. Regardless of how we got here, extinction as the destiny of man is no longer a matter of science fiction.

In work that has affected our thinking ever since, Aristotle wrote about four kinds of causes: material, formal, final, and efficient. The first three are natural phenomena of living and non-living things to be discovered by sense perception and reason. The fourth is the extra-natural cause of the other three. Aristotle's efficient cause is approached by faith and the acceptance of fundamental axioms neither directly amenable to sense perception and reason nor contradictory to them. In the eighteenth-century European "Age of Reason," an attempt at a complete separation of faith and reason, coupled with a belief in the self-sufficiency of reason to explain all causality, precipitated what Andrew White later called the "warfare of science with theology." Yet, even in Aristotle's time the ideas of Democritus and the Atomists and the reflections of Empedocles on gradual adaptation and change in organisms must have stimulated conflict between religion and natural science.

In early Christianity, St. Augustine suggested an allegorical interpretation of the Book of Genesis. More importantly, he strongly warned against the use of biblical interpretation to oppose natural science, a stance which would, Augustine believed, render the Christian a fool in the eyes of his non-Christian colleagues. Nine centuries later, St. Thomas Aquinas endorsed Augustine's views on Genesis and his unwillingness to accept a totally literal interpretation of Scripture. This Augustinian-Thomistic tradition has continued in the Roman Catholic faith, as codified in the encyclical *Humani generis* (1950), albeit with no small antagonism from some theologians and Fundamentalist Catholics.

Recently, Pierre Teilhard de Chardin's poetic works, which combine evolution and religious faith, have inspired some readers to spiritual euphoria and others to revulsion at perceived heresy, either scientific or theological. To this day the battle rages in the Roman Catholic Church.

Literal interpretation of Genesis is the basis for a body of opinion that rejects out-of-hand any evolutionary explanation of origins. The natural philosophy of the eighteenth and nineteenth centuries, like Aristotle's synthesis, included a Divine Creator or the Efficient Cause of all life forms. Building on natural philosophy, Fundamentalist thought uses the concept of fixity of species, with each "kind" created in short order from non-living matter. Orderly systems of classification established by John Ray and especially by Carolus Linnaeus in the eighteenth century Enlightenment had seemed to give scientific support to the concepts of special creation and permanence of species. In the nineteenth century, the *Bridgewater Treatises* were written by religiously motivated naturalists to explain natural phenomena in supernatural terms. The biblical Deluge and the geological catastrophism of the anti-evolutionist Georges Cuvier were invoked as causes of the massive extinction of vertebrates now known only as fossils. Noah's ark must have really contained all of the animals in existence during the Deluge. The Creation must have been completed in six solar days. The nineteenth century, however, also witnessed the rise of scientific thinking that set aside theological considerations, in favor of the Darwinian concept of adaptive change in species in response to environmental pressures.

Although Lamarck's theory of inheritance of acquired characteristics lacked support, it paved the way for Darwin's concept of evolution by natural selection of variations in populations. Even Linnaeus had second thoughts on the fixity of species because of variations within his taxonomic categories. Now the time was ripe for the biologists Darwin, Wallace, and Knight to turn the scientific world toward a concept of biological change and diversification through time as Mendel's contemporary discoveries in genetics would put the theory of evolution on a sound mathematical foundation. Geologists Lyell and Hutton gave evolution the time it needed when they demonstrated persuasively that the world was vastly older than the 6,000 years Archbishop Ussher had calculated from literal study of biblical narrative but, even as the idea of evolution gained ground, the dichotomy between religious and scientific explanations of origins was becoming more contentious.

The publication of Darwin's *Origin of Species* in 1859 was accompanied by a surge of enthusiasm from defenders and publicists whose zeal sometimes exceeded their prudence. When Thomas Henry Huxley debated with Anglican Archbishop Wilberforce, he fed the idea that religious and evolutionary explanations of origins are antagonistic if not contradictory. Ernst Haeckel spread the conflagration to Europe, and it duly crossed the Atlantic where, in 1925, America witnessed a travesty of judicial procedure. In the notorious Scopes Trial, a Tennessee teacher was prosecuted for defying a state law prohibiting the teaching of evolution. Scopes was let off on a technicality, but the law remained on the Tennessee books, though not enforced, for many years thereafter. Litigation over the teaching of evolution in schools continues to this day in the United States. Federal courts in Arkansas (1982) and Louisiana (1985) have ruled that incorporation of "creation science" into science courses is an intrusion of religious explanations into a secular subject.

Nevertheless, the debate circuit remains alive and well, with members of the Institute for Creation Research defending Creation Science, and challenging scientists of other persuasions to debate, on the premise that religious explanations of origins are as good as or better than those of evolutionary natural science.

The creation/evolution controversy may be dismissed as a confusion of two methodologies that are distinct in their protocols and objectives; the scientific method deals strictly with the "what" and "how" of origins, while the religious creation methodology deals with the "Who" and the "why." Biblical literalists insist that the Bible is an accurate scientific account of origins; scientists counter that, read literally, Genesis is incompatible with empirical findings about the natural world. If scientists discover a natural phenomenon that seemingly contradicts an interpretation of inerrant Scripture, Fundamentalists insist that their discovery must be in error. While both sides ostensibly search for truth, each suspects the other of surreptitious attempts to insinuate an ideology that furthers its own interests. Such attitudes promote selective blindness to the inherent limitations of each field of enquiry. The extension of scientific or religious concepts to social behavior is a fair example. Social Darwinism was Herbert Spencer's (*Principles of Ethics*) unjustifiable application of Darwinian principles to philosophical ethics and human behavior, resulting in such unsubstantiated, if memorable, expressions as Tennyson's "nature red in tooth and claw." By the same token, Wilson (*Sociobiology, the New Synthesis* and *On Human Nature*) is suspected of inappropriately applying biological principles of animal behavior to all aspects of human behavior.

In 1911, Henri Bergson tried to integrate scientific and philosophical viewpoints on origins in *Creative Evolution*. Bergson argued that life is a continual stream of development and diversification. His view is akin to Teilhard's (*The Future of Man*) idea of evolution toward the omega point. Where strictly literal biblical exegesis leads to contradictions of demonstrated scientific facts, and empirical science leaves us ignorant of ultimate origins and causality, theistic evolution may offer an integration—some call it a fatal compromise—of the two. One need only review the criticisms levelled against Teilhard's works as unscientific on the one hand and heretical on the other to realize that the conflict on evolution between science and religion is still raging.

While the published scientific works of Charles Darwin provide objective information on many subjects, from the pollination of orchids to the subterranean activities of earthworms, it is from his candid, informal correspondence with colleagues that we learn most about his personal convictions and how he arrived at them. The present volume of correspondence between Edward Dodson and George Howe, like Darwin's letters, preserves the relaxed qualities of discussion not originally intended for publication with the uninhibited, but charitable, enthusiasm of two thinkers with mutual agreement on some matters and diametrically opposed beliefs on others.

Both men are basically Christian by conviction and affiliation; both are professional biologists. But Dodson views Teilhard's theistic evolution as akin to his own thoughts, while Howe, the Fundamentalist, sees it as " . . . a thinly based philosophical web of factual nothingness" and tells Dodson that " . . . Teilhard looms larger in your thoughts than Moses." Dodson sees the synthesis of organic molecules from smaller ones as a step in the understanding of primordial abiogenesis; Howe calls it "Urey–Miller nonsense." Dodson accepts Scripture *and* Tradition as sources for Christian theology; Howe relies on Scripture alone. Howe considers macroevolution a philosophical concept, founded on faith; Dodson insists it is a scientific hypothesis, if not a fact. Despite the divergence of their views on the interplay of science and religion in the creation–evolution controversy, Dodson concludes that " . . . we are agreed on many articles of faith."

The title of this volume offers a choice: creation or evolution. Should the reader opt for one or the other? For both, or neither? Since issues in this controversy touch all lives in one way or another, it is impossible to remain totally neutral on them. Decisions, from the United States Supreme Court down to a local school board, affect what will be taught in public schools and which books will be made available in their libraries. Will religion be taught in science classrooms? Will religion, which has had a central role in history, have *any* place in the curriculum? Will science be subject to theological supervision and control? Will science eventually explain, or explain away, every mysterious phenomenon without recourse to miracles and the supernatural? Will ideologies, of science or religion, displace dispassionate hypotheses and theories in the search for truth?

Dodson and Howe do not provide final answers to any of these questions, but they do afford two very different viewpoints, and their contrast can enrich personal convictions on a pressing problem in contemporary society.

Lazarus Walter Macior, O.M.I., Ph.D.
Professor of Biology
University of Akron

Acknowledgments

e are indebted to many others for their assistance in bringing this correspondence to publication: Mrs. Phyllis Hughes, who typed the entire manuscript; Claude Choquette, who called the manuscript to the attention of Toivo Roht, Director of the University of Ottawa Press; Mr. Roht, for his interest in the manuscript; Mrs. Janet Shorten, English-language editor, who sponsored the book before the Publications Committee and guided it through the publication process; Mr. Peter Martin and Mrs. Jennifer Wilson, who did the editorial work; Dr. Earl Hanson, for permission to reprint his letter to the editor of *BioScience*; and Dr. Julie Ann Miller, editor of *BioScience*, for permission to reprint letters from that journal.

Edward O. Dodson
George F. Howe

Unlikely Collaborators

e, the co-authors of this book, are unlikely collaborators. One (Dodson) has had a long career in evolutionary biology, while the other (Howe) is a teaching and research biologist who is a past-president of the Creation Research Society and a past editor of the *Creation Research Society Quarterly*. We also have an important religious difference. Dodson is a practising Catholic who believes that evolution is God's method of creation of the wonderful variety of life; Howe is a fundamentalist Baptist who holds that God rapidly created many separate types of living organisms.

How did two such different people happen to collaborate? A letter to the editor of *BioScience* asked, "Why do the creationists win all the debates?" Dodson wrote an answer that was also published as a letter to the editor. Howe then wrote to Dodson to contest some of his statements. This resulted in a long correspondence in which we have discussed two principal themes: evidence for and against evolution, and the religious background of our respective positions.

We hope that these letters will interest three readerships: other fundamentalists may want to read Howe's response to the evolutionary challenge; other evolutionary scientists may want to read Dodson's response to the creationist challenge; and the interested public may want to read both sides of a controversy that has repeatedly been before legislatures and courts in recent years.

Edward O. Dodson
George F. Howe

In the Beginning . . .

(Letter to the editor, *BioScience* 30(1): 4–5, January 1980)*

W hy do creationists seem to be the consistent winners in public debates with evolutionists? That question is, for me, the most disturbing one raised by the recent article in *BioScience* by Robin Marantz Henig, entitled "Evolution called a 'Religion,' Creationism Defended as 'Science'" (see especially p. 514, first column). The apparent inadequacy of the performance by biologists is the problem I will comment on here.

In following the creationist–evolutionist controversy over the past years, I have been especially concerned with two issues on the biological side of things: first, there often still is the broad assertion, which goes beyond biology, that science and only science should appear in our science textbooks. Second, the defense of evolution is often so poorly expressed that it actually supports various criticisms that creationists have leveled at us. Both points need further elaboration.

That only science should appear in science textbooks might, at first glance, seem so obvious that further debate is unnecessary. That would be true if science did not impinge on human affairs. One measure of that impingement is the oft-used phrase "age of science," which explicitly registers the awareness that our lives are now inextricably entwined with science as a means of inquiry and as a source of powerful, usable knowledge. Future generations must be informed as never before regarding the present and potential role of science if they are responsibly to use science and its partner technology to further human welfare. A head-in-the-sand attitude that science textbooks shall contain *only* science is dangerously ill-informed regarding the need for an informed public regarding such crucial issues as pollution, population control, adequate supplies of nourishing food, nuclear energy and alternative energy technologies, genetic engineering, racism, sexism, resource management, and such confrontations as those engendered by the creationist– evolutionist issues. The input of science into these critical prob-

---

lems must be made with due regard to the strengths and limitations of science. Jack Carter raised many of the crucial issues in his article in *BioScience* (29: 478–481, August 1979). Here I would only add that we must realize that science is a tripartite entity: it is a way to ask and answer questions; it is the product of that inquiry, namely, a body of knowledge; and it is a social institution, a group of humans who are part of the society within which they live and function as scientists. This tripartite view of science makes more explicit the difficulties and opportunities that need to be met in responsibly and credibly melding science into society.

To present evolutionary thought effectively, biologists must recognize precisely the structure of scientific knowledge as it derives from scientific inquiry. We must put a stop to false claims such as "evolution is a fact" or that science can "prove" this or that explanation. As one who subscribes to Dobzhansky's[1] dictum "that nothing in biology makes sense except in the light of evolution," and as a teacher of and researcher in evolutionary biology, I yield to no one in my respect for evolutionary thought and science in general. But that knowledge must be handled credibly and responsibly. Therefore, regarding the claim that evolution is a fact, we should note the following points. In Darwinian terms, evolution refers to changes accumulated by natural selection in living things, especially regarding species formation. Furthermore, this whole process is rarely observed directly; for that reason alone, it is hardly factual. It is a reconstruction from facts. More significantly, evolution is often confused with natural selection. How often do we hear of "Darwin's theory of evolution" or simply "the theory of evolution"? Darwin's theory is that of natural selection; the operation of natural selection causes evolution. A cause and its effect can never be the same thing.

Even if we overlook the foregoing source of confusion and accept that evolution is unfortunately used in two ways—i.e., synonymous with natural selection (a causal theory) and with accumulated evolutionary change (the consequence of the theory)—we are still nowhere near justifying the statement that "evolution is a fact." The facts in the study of evolution come from the observed variations and differences among organisms. Those facts are to be understood as the result of changes preserved by natural selection. There has occurred here a confusion between the problem—the facts of organic diversity—and the explanation of the problem—the theory of evolutionary change through natural selection. Facts are descriptive statements; theories are explanatory ones; they can never be equated.

The notion that science "proves" theories comes from the same muddled school of thought. Science tests its hypotheses and *disproves* the wrong ones. Progress in science (a complex topic today in the history and philosophy of science) is essentially limited to culling out the deadwood of mistaken explanations (theories and hypotheses). This can be shown by practising simple logic.

The logic of the situation tells us a true hypothesis results in a true prediction and experimental results that fulfill the prediction (they, too, are true). But a false hypothesis can produce equivocal results. Thus, we cannot identify a true hypothesis simply because predicted results are observed (i.e., we cannot prove a true explanation). We can, however, disprove a false hypothesis because false or unexpected experimental results occur unequivocally as a consequence of a false hypothesis. Of course, we are dealing with the "logic of the situation"; human experimental error is another, but separate, complication. Hence, the underlying logic of scientific inquiry demands that we forgo the notion that science can prove its hypotheses or explanatory statements.

These comments obviously only hint at the complexity of the issues involved here, but my intent is, I hope, clear enough: we biologists are our own worst enemies in the creationist–evolutionist controversies. We must no longer duck this and other issues related to biology and human affairs, and when we do face them we must think clearly and express ourselves accordingly. We may still not be consistent winners in the creationist–evolutionist debates, but let the losses that occur be attributable to other than lapses in professional standards.

Earl D. Hanson
College of Science in Society
Wesleyan University
Middletown, CT 06457

(Letter to the editor, *BioScience* 30(4): 220–221, April 1980)*

I would like to comment on Hanson's letter on the evolution/creation debate (*BioScience* 30: 4–5, January 1980). He asks, "Why do creationists seem to be the consistent winners in public debates with evolutionists?" In part, his answer is that we are careless with our definitions. I am sure that this is often true, but does Hanson really believe that the creationists are better off in this respect? They may, indeed, be worse off and still win the debates.

An important factor is the nature of a debate before a non-professional audience. I present my course in evolution to students who have already had courses in genetics, cell biology, botany, zoology, comparative anatomy, embryology, physiology, and ecology, as well as an introduction to chemistry, biochemistry, physics, calculus, statistics, and often other applicable sciences such as geology. When I discuss an example from these fields, the students are able to evaluate it as part of a systematic field of knowledge rather than as an isolated curiosity. The intellectual value of the course in evolution derives in important part from its role as a synthesis of all aspects of biology and of much from other sciences as well.

In a public debate, it is impossible to assume that the audience is biologically well informed. It is necessary to start from the beginning and, in the brief time at the debater's disposal, he cannot go very far unless he treats the subject very superficially. If he chooses to develop a very small part of the subject in depth, he will probably soon go beyond the capacity of an untrained audience to follow technical reasoning in biology. If he prefers a broad survey of the subject, then the superficiality that the circumstances impose provides an easy target for his opponent. Thus, the evolutionist in public debate is on the horns of a dilemma.

The debater for creationism suffers no such liability. He usually does not attempt to present a systematic argument in

---

favor of special creation. Rather, he picks flaws in the argument for evolution, then concludes that, because the argument for evolution is so defective, that for special creation must be right.

The flaws that the creationists exploit are in some cases real, but in others they are based upon failure to understand the biological data (or the biologist). In public debates, the difference is not important, because the audience is unlikely to recognize it. In some cases, it is the biologist's frank recognition of unsolved problems or of limitations of knowledge that provides the target for the creationist. Thus, we commonly emphasize unsolved problems partly to avoid giving the impression that all of the problems are tidily solved and partly to call attention to areas where research is needed. I have before me a creationist leaflet. It lists quotations from Julian Huxley, R. E. Leakey, A. S. Romer, G. G. Simpson, G. L. Stebbins, and other evolutionary biologists. Each quotation concerns some flaw, lacuna, or limitation in evolutionary science. Quoted out of context, they suggest that the leading proponents of evolution are on the verge of abandoning it. Readers of *BioScience* know that this is a gross misconstruction, but biologically untrained audiences are impressed.

Perhaps the basic problem is that public debate is simply not an appropriate method for resolving scientific issues. Of the many controversial issues with which biologists have dealt recently, none has been resolved by public debate. The ordinary method has been research to test hypotheses and publication of the results in refereed journals, where the reports are subject to criticism by the scientific peers of the authors. This may lead to further publications—either to corroborate or to contest the data and explanatory theories put forward. All may be discussed at scientific meetings and in seminars, and a consensus may be reached among scientific peers.

The creationists currently claim that they are working scientists in such fields as genetics, embryology, comparative anatomy, and biochemistry. If this is correct, then they should be able to publish, in refereed journals, the results of investigations that they think favor special creation rather than evolution. If they could submit even minimally creditable papers, I believe that most editors would bend over backwards to find space for them. However, I am yet to see the first such paper.

Further, I think that every invitation to debate should be refused on the grounds that debate is not a suitable method for resolving scientific questions. If the creationists are serious about their claim to genuine status in science, refereed publication is the only way to give substance to that claim and to earn a place of respect in the scientific community.

In short, they should put up or shut up.

Edward Dodson
Department of Biology
University of Ottawa

The Letters

April 23, 1980

Dear Dr. Dodson:

Enclosed please find a letter which I have submitted to *BioScience* in answer to one or two of the points you raised in your previous letter.

It may surprise you to learn that, at Westmont College in Santa Barbara when I was a very young teacher (1959, 1960, etc.), I used your textbook on evolution as the key text in an "Origins" course I taught there. I found the book helpful and quite representative in expressing the current evolutionary thought.

You also may be surprised to learn that I agree with your "put up or shut up" philosophy as regards creationists. Please let me know your exact field of speciality and I will be willing to Xerox several key papers in that area for you from the *CRSQ* to demonstrate that the kind of thing you are looking for does exist. I am somewhat saddened by the fact that a man of your scientific stature did not investigate this matter more fully before publishing a letter which appears to be more emotionally and philosophically based than it is scientific in its content. In light of what I am bringing to your attention, you might want to consider publishing a retraction of your remarks.

The reason we are willing to debate evolutionists is that it is quite easy to show that the neo-Darwinian model is relatively indefensible. However, like you, I personally shun debates because I believe they present a poor teaching format and, like you again, I believe that ultimately scientific models must stand or fall on their fit with extant data and not on the showmanship of the debaters involved. Thus, I have participated in only four debates in the last ten years or so. I go to debates only when I am requested and I do not seek these opportunities out, for the reasons indicated. Personally, however, if you do not believe that it is easy to demonstrate the scientific inadequacies of our current evolution model and to make a case to show that many of the data of science have good fit with the creation science model, I will be happy to carry out extensive personal correspondence with you.

Sincerely yours,

George F. Howe

[Submitted for possible publication in "Letters to the editor" in response to E. O. Dodson]

Creationist-based Research Papers

If Dr. Edward O. Dodson, in his letter on the evolution/creation debate (*BioScience* 30(4): 220–221, April 1980) is really looking for data-based, peer-reviewed research papers by scientifically minded special creationists, he should have looked in the pages of the *Creation Research Society Quarterly* [*CRSQ*], which is presently (in 1980) in its seventeenth year of publication. Authors of numerous *CRSQ* papers have covered many aspects of the classical origins debate, as is evident in the following examples:

Gish, D. T. October 1964. "A critique of biochemical evolution." *CRSQ* 1(2): 10–12. (Note: Dr. Gish is a highly qualified chemist who has published many other articles since this date, but this reference indicates just how far back into the literature such papers go.)

Howe, G. F. March 1976. "Post-fire regrowth of *Adenostoma fasciculatum* H. & A. and *Ceanothus crassifolius* Torr. in relation to ecology and origins." *CRSQ* 12(4): 184–190. (Note: I am a physiological ecologist.)

Lammerts, W. E. May 1965. "Planned induction of commercially desirable variation in roses by neutron radiation." *CRSQ* 2(1): 39–48. (Note: Dr. Lammerts is a geneticist and rose-breeder with many "All American" rose selection awards to his credit.)

Nevins, S. E. March 1972. "Is the Capitan Limestone a fossil reef?" *CRSQ* 8(4): 231–238. (Note: "Stuart E. Nevins" is a pen name adopted by Steven Austin, a coal geologist presently with the Institute for Creation Research in San Diego.)

Smith, E. N. March 1979. "Marine life and the flood." *CRSQ* 15(4): 179–183. (Note: E. N. Smith is a highly published reptile physiologist and this paper concerns survival of both fresh- and salt-water species in the same global catastrophe. It is a report on laboratory experiments involving fish.)

The *CRSQ* may be purchased by writing to the Membership Secretary.

If Dr. Dodson wonders why these data papers and others like them were not published in some other peer-review journals, he would be surprised to find out what sort of treatment creationist papers receive at the hands of evolution-minded referees. One might also ask why the current abstracting services such as *Biological Abstracts* are not including abstracts of these and other research papers published in *CRSQ*.

The answer is obvious.

George Howe
President and editor, Creation Research Society [CRS]

May 6, 1980

Dear Dr. Howe:

Thank you for your letter of April 23, and for the enclosure which you sent to *BioScience*. I hope and expect that *BioScience* will publish it. I was not familiar with the *Creation Research Society Quarterly*, and I suspect that I am not alone in this respect among the readers of *BioScience*. It is not in our library, and there is little possibility of our adding it, as we are faced with austerity budgeting. It may be in the National Science Library. I will check the next time I visit NSL.

I am pleased to learn that you used my book on evolution some years ago, and that you found it useful. My son (a vertebrate paleontologist) and I updated it in 1976. Perhaps you may. again find it useful. In presenting my own course, I tell the students that, if they have religious convictions opposed to evolution, I have no interest in shaking those convictions. I, too, have strong religious convictions. But, as most biologists regard evolution as one of the most important biological generalizations, students of biology should know why most biologists think as they do. Perhaps you agree.

I am also pleased to learn that you agree with my "put up or shut up" philosophy, although I feel a bit chagrined that I didn't find a less provocative phrase. You asked for my field of specialization. I started out as a cytologist working on lampbrush chromosomes, but I soon got shunted into genetics. I am interested in mutation and population genetics, always from an evolutionary viewpoint. In recent years, I have also worked on broad taxonomy (how many kingdoms, and what relationships among them).

You were saddened because my letter to *BioScience* was ". . . more emotionally and philosophically based than it is scientific . . . ." On rereading it, I find little emotional content except for the final line, about which I am not happy. There are many definitions of philosophy, most of which will not satisfy a philosopher. One such is that philosophy is a broad view of a subject. My letter might qualify as philosophical under that definition. It was a reply to Hanson's letter, and as such I think that it was appropriate. I introduced no new scientific data, and I do not believe that that was called for.

You cite a number of published papers, and suggest that I may want to publish a retraction because of this. You add, however, "If Dr. Dodson wonders why these . . . were not published in some other peer-review journals . . . ." I do, indeed, and I appreciate your problem; yet I don't believe that the inferred answer is adequate. It would not be very helpful if I were to publish a retraction and add the qualification that some of the papers should have been published elsewhere. The main reason is that most other scientists simply will not see papers which are published in *CRSQ*. To reach a broad scientific readership, you must publish in journals which other scientists read. There are several reasons why I believe that this is feasible in spite of the anti-creationist bias of referees. I am thinking of my highly respected colleague, Vadim D. Vladykov,[2] the Dean of ichthyologists of the world. As a very devout Russian Orthodox, he has never accepted evolution. Throughout his long career (he is in his eighties), he has published much in the best journals. His papers are not concerned with origins. They deal with taxonomy and various aspects of fish ecology. But, if he chooses to comment on origins, all ichthyologists will listen respectfully, because he has established his authority beyond dispute.

Similarly, H. J. Muller recognized very early in his career that he must *first establish his authority as a geneticist if he wanted to get a hearing for his more controversial ideas*. He set about a systematic program of research and publication which established his scientific authority so well that he was awarded a Nobel prize. Only after he had gained international repute did he start publishing his controversial eugenic ideas.

In other words, factual presentation of scientific results comes first, controversial conclusions later. If you and your colleagues were to follow this route, you might find that you could establish a degree of scientific credibility which would make it easier for you to get a hearing for creationism.

Your letter included some surprises for me, and perhaps I have some for you. The first is that I am not and never have been a convinced neo-Darwinian. I did my doctoral studies under Richard Goldschmidt, who was much resented by the neo-Darwinians. In my book, I tried to present alternative theories and to call attention to deficiencies, and I was severely criticized by some of the neo-Darwinians because of this.

Second, you may be surprised that I consider myself a creationist. I am a thoroughly convinced Catholic, and I believe that the entire phenomenal universe is God's handiwork. I believe, however, that He ordinarily works through natural processes, including evolution for the creation of the world of life.

Again, thank you for your letter.

Sincerely yours,

Edward O. Dodson
Professor of Biology

June 2, 1980

Dear Dr. Dodson:

Thanks for your kindness in replying so promptly to my earlier letter. Actually, *BioScience* will not be publishing my letter, as Mr. Peter indicated to me, not because they care to squelch the issue but because they have already published several articles by both creationists and evolutionists and feel they must close the issue at this point. I can understand this type of editorial decision because I was for five years the editor of *CRSQ*.

If I may be so bold as to suggest this, let me encourage you to get a subscription to *CRSQ*. Perhaps with some prodding your own library committee can be convinced it is time to include this despite monetary constraints. Perhaps you will consider purchasing it yourself and donating it to the library. Anyway, I believe that, as a long-time student of origins, you would find the issues quite illuminating as to current creationist thought. Here, of course, I am distinguishing between creationists such as yourself, who hold that the Creator worked by evolution, and "special creationists," who hold that there is evidence to believe that there was a "fiat" or rapid aspect in keeping with the Judeo-Christian concept of "miracles" seen in the Genesis 1–2[3] creation account (cf. Exodus 20:11), as well as in other critical periods in earth's history such as the Mosaic exodus, the days of the prophets, and at the birth of Our Lord who came via God-ordained parthenogenesis and who, of course, arose physically from the tomb with a resurrection body.

I am not altogether surprised to learn that you are a Christian and a "creationist" in the sense of "theistic evolution." Dobzhansky likewise held, I believe, to a God-directed scheme of evolution as Theodosius had earlier begun to study in the Russian Orthodox Church. Most of my Roman Catholic friends in "academia" are theistic evolutionists. Along that line, I am including a theological-scientific paper of mine about miracles in creation. While it is quite true that God COULD have created any way He had wished, a question Bible students must answer is how DID God create and what did He TELL us as regards the process. It is right here that you as a Catholic would have a sensitivity that many of our philosophically "naturalistic" friends would lack. Careful study of documents demonstrates that there was a miraculous and short-term component described in the Bible creation accounts which has unfortunately been abandoned by many Catholics and Protestants. I trust you will be interested in my paper on miracles.

Perhaps right here I should make my own theological underpinnings known. I probably cannot be classified as "Protestant" or "Catholic" in the older sense of those terms. In fact, I have found so much emphasis in the gospels and the epistles upon coming to know Jesus Christ as personal savior and Lord through faith that I am into what can be classified as the "born again" phase of contemporary theology. I am a Baptist, of course, but feel that the main thrust of Our Lord's ministry was to seek out people who would profess Him as their personal savior and sin-bearer. Since I have taken this step of faith, I have discovered forgiveness for my sin and am guaranteed a future life with God as we learn from John 3:16, 1 John 4:15, and Romans 10:9 and 10, for example. I know some Roman Catholics who have taken this same step of personal faith and I count them brothers and sisters in Christ. I know some Baptists who reject the saving grace of Christ and, unfortunately, the Bible says they are lost, whatever their label.

We have both been in for surprises and I may be giving you one now when I admit that I likewise believe the Creator ordinarily works by what you call "natural processes." These are, of course, not "natural" in the sense that they go on apart from God's control but are simply His "usual" way of working. After all, the Creator works much the same way that the apostle recommended to early Christians: "Let everything be done decently and in order." The spot where we probably part company at present is that I believe the Creator did use miracles at several key junctures in the history of life and man. One of these, I am sure we both agree, came at the time that the Holy Spirit miraculously induced the conception of a virgin-born male— Jesus the Christ who was both God and perfect man. Likewise, we realize that, whatever "miracles" are, they were involved at the time that Jesus arose from the tomb to the great surprise of both His friends and His enemies. But even further, Dr. Dodson, you will discover, in studying Genesis in its own light as well as in the writings of old Catholic theologians, that there is a miraculous component involved in creating the universe, the world, plants, animals, and man in six real days. Once again, I invite your attention to my paper on miracles.

Now all of this would be very one-sided and very puzzling if "religion" on the one side were asking that the earth, etc. be created recently and rapidly while "science" on the other were to show vast arrays of evidence in clear support of a developmental creation across long ages of time. In fact, no such dichotomy exists. There is no scientific evidence that confirms more than a few slight species changes. There is no unequivocal barrage of data to shoot down the special creationists' contention that the earth is very young. There is no "science" of time when we realize that written records go back only a few short thousands of years. The radioactive dating schemes are each based on several unsupported and unsupportable assumptions. The dating methods conflict among themselves and those dates which do not fit the preconceived ideas of evolution-minded paleontologists are discarded or rationalized.

I am fascinated, of course, by your broad background in genetics. The fact that you always studied genetics "from an evolutionary viewpoint" puzzles me. Perhaps even now you owe it to yourself to view the genetic evidence which conflicts with evolution theories (theistic or naturalistic evolution). You see, there is nothing wrong with a creationist stressing the weaknesses in the evolution model. If a faulty model is to be replaced with an effective one, the advocates of the newer model must do two things: (1) they must show that there is sufficient weakness in the established view to merit rethinking and to merit consideration of alternatives; (2) they must show how a particular alternative model fits with the existing data of the natural sciences. Thus, it is a legitimate task of the creationist to spend considerable time stressing the weaknesses and downright flaws in evolutionary fabric—I believe you objected to all of this in your article.

If there are flaws with the evolution model, then we had better "out" with it—in public and in private conversation. To do otherwise would be to make the evolution model into some kind of reverent object which is beyond the pale of evaluation and criticism. Kerkut did not recommend this. He asked his early students in college to spend as much time studying the problems of evolution theory as they did its supposed strengths.

I am not sure I understand some of your comments. Surely you do not mean to imply that you are unwilling to discuss the problems of the evolution model seriously until your students are indoctrinated in all the courses you indicated? I must have misunderstood your thrust and will appreciate clarification. Is the evolution model so involved (esoteric?) and so abstract that it cannot be defended effectively before a public audience? Are you actually disturbed when the flaws in this theory which you favor are publicly aired? Surely I misinterpret what you wrote because you must admit that every theory deserves to be tested and evaluated continually and that good models must be so well based in experimental data that they can be verified or falsified for public view.

Now this leads to some comment on other points in your fine letter. I hope you are not intending to commit two logical fallacies at once. You know of course about the fallacy of the *argumentum ad hominem*? You come very close to committing this when you demand that no one criticize evolution or speak openly about alternative origins models unless they first distinguish themselves in original research in one of the related fields. If a plumber or bricklayer can pick up books on origins and see flaws in the use of data, they deserve a hearing. You must remember that there is an indoctrination effect which pervades many fields. Frequently it almost demands someone from outside the establishment to bring fresh ideology. Thus, Charles Darwin's education was not in biology but in theology. Lyell was a lawyer, not a trained geologist. William Smith was a canal engineer, not a geologist by training, and the list could go on. Surely we must take arguments on their own merit and not exact academic pedigrees out of people who ask intelligent questions or suggest changes?

Next, in your letter you continue by indicating that somehow Muller began speaking about controversial things such as eugenics after he had had a powerful career in biology. The inference is that we should pay attention to his political philosophy in the domain of eugenics because he was so good at studying mutations in *Drosophila*. Let me quickly state that this borders on the "halo effect" which is so grossly applied in the world of commercial advertising. If Linus Pauling is a good chemist, should I listen to him when it comes to consuming 5 grams of ascorbic acid every day? If "X" is a very great athlete, should I drink his same brand of beer or even drink beer at all just because he does?

With all of this behind, let me state once again that I believe it is *ideal* and that it is *best* for creationists to engage themselves quite actively in basic research. I will furthermore agree with you that we special creationists should seek to publish in journals other than *CRSQ*. However, does this excuse our evolution-minded cohorts from failing to purchase and read *CRSQ*? Does it excuse *BioAbstracts* from failing to print a precis of each *CRSQ* data paper? Surely they know the journal exists.

Presently I have a data paper in press with the Southern California Academy of Sciences; it is slated to appear in their first 1980 issue. After this paper appears, I want to publish a paper that is oriented to origins discussion of the creation model, based on my own findings and on the work of two of the people in my references. I would like to get this paper into the journal *Evolution*. Right here is where you figure into the equation. Would you be willing to read my original research papers, and then read the paper that I produce on a special creationist view of origins and serve as a referee? If we can come up with a paper that you feel takes data and interprets them in keeping with a special creationist format in a legitimate fashion, would you be willing to support the publication of my paper in the journal *Evolution*? I wouldn't be asking that you agree with the paper— merely that you criticize it, after which I will rewrite according to your suggestions, and then that you help me get it published. Several times our special creationist authors have approached *Evolution* editors with papers that were flatly rejected and we later published these valuable papers in *CRSQ*. One case in point is the paper by Dr. John N. Moore, published in 1973, which showed that most of the papers in the *Evolution* journal do not deal with "evolution" in the broader sense, but only with minor changes that creationists and all others recognize in the world of nature.

I gave a paper on parallelisms in botany at the American Biology Teachers Association in 1972 in San Francisco and they did not publish that paper. Sir, you have not lived on the other side of this question and you have not experienced the absolute dogmatic fixity with which many evolutionists reject any papers which include creationist ideology.

We are in trouble either way. People like yourself, who assume that we would receive fair treatment, tell us to begin publishing our data papers along with our creationist models in the usual journals. But as soon as this is tried, referees and editors brush off our papers as "non-scientific" and unfit for their journals. Believe me when I say that I would like to over- come the obstacle even more than you who give us advice from the outside.

Despite all this, many of our people are doing exactly what Vladykov did. Perhaps you do not realize that Dr. Walter E. Lammerts is presently revered as the "Father of Modern Rose- breeding." Perhaps you are likewise unaware that his rose Queen Elizabeth recently was voted the world's most popular rose. Maybe you have overlooked the fact that Dr. Duane Gish participated in a very effective research team in virus biochem- istry both at Stanford and Cornell universities. These people and scores like them ARE publishing data papers in the field and ARE becoming known as giants of research, while at the same time they publish creation-oriented papers in *CRSQ* and in other journals as editors will permit. In essence, what you asked in your letter to the editor has already been happening. Creation-oriented science is on the upsurge.

You are correct in maintaining that your letter to the editor was not as "emotional" as I had suggested in my letter. Upon a rereading of your published letter, however, it appears that you came very close to saying that evolution theory is only for the elite or the indoctrinated and that its advocates are not very well able to defend it in the public market of discussion.

Let me repeat, I usually avoid debates for the same reasons you do. But I believe the reason evolutionists routinely appear to lose debates is that they have a very hard theory to defend. Thermodynamically it is bizarre, to say the least. Genetically it is unlikely that adaptation will arise via small changes, most of which are deleterious. Congratulations on including the late and great Dr. Goldschmidt's views in your textbook. I remember that, as well as the fact that you included the problems facing evolution theorists at different junctures in paleontology. May I also make another point? You are an exception when it comes to evolution theory in that you are a theist, and will admit this—at least in private correspondence. One of the strongest arguments favoring the creation view (theistic or special creationism) is the argument of DESIGN in nature. This supports divine intervention (either gradually or rapidly) but why are evolutionists generally so unwilling to grant this (if they believe it) or even to discuss it if they object?

How can one explain the chance origin of DNA and the correct DNA polymerases to function within the cell? DNA, of course, cannot reproduce in an orderly fashion without just the right polymerase. But, by the same token, the polymerase cannot be translated if appropriate mRNA has not been transcribed from just the right DNA (gene) to produce the polymerase. Here we have the old "which came first, the chicken or the egg?" problem with a vengeance. It is obvious that neither one came first but both arose AT ONCE. Why are evolutionists so adamant about refusing to discuss all of this in the context of science? Surely we can discuss Shakespeare while we analyze his sonnets or great plays? Is it not gross plagiarism to ignore this kind of evidence (as our secular evolutionists do) while at the same time we rejoice in analyzing the Creator's handiwork?

I wish to thank you once again for the friendly tone of your letter. Frequently I find that evolutionists will not even answer my letters. I trust that, as time permits, we may continue our correspondence. I am enclosing some papers for your analysis, and you may surely keep these for your files on special creationism. I respect the way you deal with students—suggesting that, if they have "religious" convictions against evolution, you are not interested to shake them. What I am trying to stress in our conversations, however, is that many students and many of your professional colleagues have scientific as well as religious objections to this model.

Best personal regards,

George F. Howe

June 30, 1980

Dear Dr. Howe:

You may find this letter something of a disappointment, as I shall not attempt to answer your letter in full. Such voluminous correspondence (five typed pages, single-spaced!) is extremely time-consuming, and could easily prevent us both from giving adequate attention to our other duties. Further, you earned a Ph.D. in plant physiology at Ohio State, and you have read my book, and I have read many presentations of the thesis of special creation; hence, I am sure that we are familiar with much the same array of data on both sides of the issue. We simply evaluate it differently. As each of us is confirmed in his viewpoint, neither is very likely to change. We both know the arguments on the other side and, for reasons which each of us considers adequate, we reject them. I shall therefore confine myself to a few comments on specific points in your letter.

Your paper on miracles has not arrived, but I will read it with interest. We are in complete agreement that miracles do occur. We may differ as to whether a miracle has occurred in specific instances. We are in agreement that natural processes are what they are because that is the way that God ordinarily works. This in itself makes it difficult to define "miracles," yet we can agree that many events in the life of Our Lord, and most especially His conception and resurrection, fulfill any possible definition. I am not so sure that that is necessarily true of the first two chapters of Genesis. As you say, many of the older Catholic theologians (and even some contemporary ones) so interpreted it, but not all: St. Augustine interpreted Genesis along lines quite congenial to evolution. The alternative simply was not presented to the older theologians in a meaningful way.

We are all "born of water and the Spirit" through baptism but, as you know, the "born again" phase of contemporary theology gives this a special meaning which most Catholics do not follow. On the other hand, devout Catholics have always had a strongly personal faith in Christ. In my letter to *BioScience*, it was not my intention to suggest that evolution should not be criticized. In my book and in my course, I give a lot of attention to the problems and criticisms. As in any scientific course, I try to indicate the areas that need more research. If you read the letter as a whole, I think that you will see that I was not protesting criticism, but was simply giving an alternative answer to Hanson's question. No, I do not regard evolution as an esoteric subject. However, it must be discussed in terms of specific data. One of the important aspects of modern evolutionary science is that it has become a synthesis of all aspects of biology and of some other sciences as well. Its data are drawn from all of these, and of course it can be best understood by students who already have a rich background in biological sciences. Would you discuss calculus with students who had not yet studied arithmetic, algebra, and trigonometry?

I agree with you that advances in any field are sometimes blocked by professional prejudices and may be catalyzed by a keen, well-informed mind from outside the discipline. Generally, however, these "catalysts" are well prepared by related studies or experience. To take only one example, you mention that Charles Darwin was a theology student. True, but he had had a hobby of natural history throughout childhood; he had studied medicine at Edinburgh; he had participated in natural science organizations at both Edinburgh and Cambridge and had read research papers to these societies; he had attracted the friendship and the coaching of distinguished men of science at the universities; he had for five years been the working naturalist on the *Beagle* and, after the return of the *Beagle*, he had concentrated upon scientific work for twenty years before the publication of the *Origin*, during which time he had achieved international status as a scientist by publication of his geological works and the four-volume treatise on the *Cirripedia*, a work which is still the necessary starting point for any serious study of this group.

You ask whether I would be willing to read a paper which you are planning and to help you prepare it for publication in *Evolution*. I would be glad to read it and to give you my suggestions on what revisions may be needed to make it acceptable to the editor. I would be glad to do the best that I can, but you must know that I am not a botanist, and much less a plant physiologist. You also ask whether I would be willing to act as a referee. Again, I would be willing, but the editor usually names the referees and does not disclose their identity to the author. At the outset, I would advise that the data be new observations, and that the conclusions be no more than are actually required by the data.

I am glad to learn from your letter that many creationists are in fact publishing in the ordinary journals of science and are gaining substantial recognition as scientists. As I do not follow the literature of rose-breeding, I am not familiar with Dr. Lammerts, but I do not find him listed in *American Men and Women of Science*, as he should be if he has the reputation which you say he does. I had heard that Dr. Gish had done excellent work in biochemistry, but again I am a little shocked to find him unlisted.

One final comment. With regard to evolution, you remark that "Thermodynamically it is bizarre, to say the least." This is a criticism which has not gone unnoticed by students of evolution. In a word, I do not believe that it is a valid criticism. I am enclosing a couple of pages Xeroxed from an unpublished book of mine[4] in which you will find my views on this subject. I believe that this is typical of our differences of evaluation of the same array of data.

Enough of this. I look forward to seeing the paper which you are preparing for *Evolution*.

Sincerely yours,

Edward O. Dodson
Professor of Biology

July 4, 1980

Dear Dr. Howe:

Greetings on your national holiday! We had ours three days ago.

I have been sampling the collection of papers which you sent me, and I have read a few of them carefully. I would like to comment on two of them. I really don't think that it is necessary to appeal to editorial prejudice to understand why these papers were rejected by the editors of the journals to which they were submitted.

First, John N. Moore's paper, "Retrieval system problems with articles in *Evolution*." This is the type of library research which *Evolution* has never published, regardless of the viewpoint of the author. The only place for it in *Evolution*, without a radical change of editorial policy, would be in the "Notes and Comments" section, and it is far too long for that, as the section is restricted to very short papers. Further, I suspect that a disinterested person would consider the frequency of use of the word "evolution" to be of little importance. Darwin rarely, if ever, used it, yet no one would suggest that he didn't write about it. As Dr. Lammerts might say, "A rose by any other name smells as sweet." Moore defines evolution in a way which restricts it to macroevolution; then he says that most of the articles in *Evolution* do not treat evolution because they are concerned with various aspects of microevolution. As the editors and contributors use definitions of evolution which are more inclusive, they consider that these papers do deal with evolution. Moore's point is merely a semantic one and, in my opinion, not a very good one.

Nonetheless, I think that Moore's article contains a kernel which might have been publishable in *Evolution* ("Notes and Comments") had it been properly presented. First, it would require condensation to "Notes and Comments" dimensions. Over half of the article is tabular, and all of that should be eliminated and summarized tersely. He could state that tabulation of all of the articles in vols. 1–25 had shown that xx% of them dealt with microevolution, and that the majority of these articles were possible within the framework of creationism. He might even give a few references to comparable papers which had been written by creationists. In this way, he could have made his basic point and made it where he would reach the desired readership.

Second, let me comment on your own paper on "Homology, Analogy, and Innovative Teaching." As I rarely see *NABT*,[5] I am less well prepared to guess what the editor's reaction might be. However, if I were the editor, I would suggest pruning much material which doesn't bear closely upon the concepts of homology and analogy. As Linnaeus and Cuvier both preceded Owen by many years, they might be tersely treated as forerunners. It is always tempting to a writer to enlarge on his subject, but most editors prefer condensation. After all, they work with limited space and funds. Finally, I would like to ask you to compare your paper with three others. Two of these are your papers from the *Ohio Journal of Science* which you sent me. As I am not even remotely a plant physiologist, you may place more value on someone else's evaluation; yet they impress me as excellent examples of good scientific writing. The third is a paper by Carl Hubbs which treats your subject. Hubbs' paper comes to grips with these concepts in a fashion which I think you will admire, and which I missed in your paper. I think that, if you will read all four papers comparatively, you will understand why the editor of *NABT* rejected your paper.

I know that these criticisms may hurt, but please believe that they are intended to be helpful, and that they are offered in a friendly spirit.

Sincerely yours,

Edward O. Dodson

July 30, 1980

Dear Dr. Dodson:

Thanks for the careful answers you attempted to give to issues raised in my letters. I shall sometime prepare a paper for *Evolution* magazine, as discussed, and I appreciate your willingness to give pointers. If *Evolution* magazine has a policy of publishing data papers to the exclusion of review papers such as Dr. Moore's, then it is not clear to me why a paper like the one I enclose herewith was ever published. Is it possible that they hold to such a policy with rigidity when approached by creationists but with latitude when it concerns evolutionary papers?

I appreciate your desire not to become encumbered with a long and exhausting routine of correspondence. I agree. Let's just keep the channels of communication open so that, whenever we produce papers that might be of significance to the other, we may send them.

Please consider having the University of Ottawa purchase *CRSQ* for their library. My students read *Evolution*; do yours read *CRSQ*? Surely people at large secular institutions can afford to be as broad and open in their treatment of controversial matters as we poor obscurantists at the parochial colleges.

I am enclosing some things herewith that might interest you: (1) a reinterpretation of data bearing on the origin of cultivated plants, by Lammerts and me; (2) a paper on your own beloved ideas of endosymbiosis as a putative scheme for the origin of mitochondria and chloroplasts—a matter that is fraught with hopeless problems—by Raff and Mahler; (3) a paper from *Evolution* magazine showing they do publish strictly review papers; (4) a paper of my own showing that I too have got onto the Goedel theorem as regards origins.

Several months after the editors of *BioScience* told me my letter would not be published because they had cut off debate on origins three weeks earlier, they recently (July) printed a strongly biased letter by Sidney Fox. Evidently they closed the issue of origins just about long enough to reject my letter. Is this but another example of the objectivity you assured me we creationists would receive from our evolution-oriented colleagues?

I value your ideas. Thanks for the generous and cordial spirit manifest in your correspondence. Write whenever you wish but never feel obligated to answer. Keep me on the mailing list for your new papers—I am enjoying the study of the ones you have sent.

With best regards,

George F. Howe

August 19, 1980

Dear Dr. Howe:

Thank you for your letter and enclosure of July 30. It was waiting for me when I returned yesterday from my vacation. Thanks, too, for the copy of your letter to the editor of *BioScience*. Incidentally, I did not say, in my letter to the editor, that creationists had been unable to produce ". . . even minimally creditable papers . . . ." I said that, if they were to submit such papers, "I believe that most editors would bend over backwards to find space for them." Obviously, the editor of *BioScience* did not try very hard to find space for your letter, and I am frankly surprised. I think that he should have published your letter.

On the other hand, I did not say that John N. Moore's paper on "Retrieval system problems . . ." was rejected because *Evolution* does not publish reviews. Of course, they have published many reviews. I said that the paper is the type of library research which they have never published (even on the side of evolution). If you will reread paragraphs 3 and 4 of my letter of July 4, I think that you will find that my comments are not recognizable in terms of your letter of July 30. Further, I did give specific suggestions (paragraph 4) for revisions which might have made Moore's paper acceptable to the editor of *Evolution*. Until and unless such revisions are made, I must continue to believe that Moore has not submitted "a minimally creditable paper," and I do not believe that you have given a relevant reply to that criticism.

Yes, by all means let us keep the lines of communication open.

Sincerely yours,

Edward O. Dodson

October 31, 1980

Dear Dr. Dodson:

Thank you for sending me a copy of your recently edited book *Viewpoints on Evolution and Religion*. You are to be highly commended for having invited people to write who differ dramatically from your own stance on origins—witness the clearly written paper by Sylvia Clarence-Smith who "hits the nail right on the head" regarding proper portrayal of a fundamentalist view of evolution.

I have read certain of the other essays—Kratky on the communist view, James Henry's biased mouthings, and Donald Champagne, who correctly scores Duane Gish for failing to recognize the Gunflint as containing some Pre-Cambrian fossils, but who also exposes his own ignorance in the area of vertebrate paleontology. I shall read all of the others as time permits. Thank you for sending this material. Also, I appreciate the way you have extended the bibliography to include works by Morris and Clark. I might suggest that you investigate the statement that J. C. Greene represents "Protestant" thought. I have read two of John's books and from all I could tell he represents NO religious position or at least not one of the usual religious positions. H. W. Clark is a Seventh-Day Adventist and would thus be considered "Protestant," I guess. Furthermore, Clark has a fine book, *Fossils, Flood, and Fire*, a work which is still in print. Clark is a geologist who defends the flood-geological model.

One good turn deserves another. Since I sense that you are a student of Teilhard, I wonder if you have read a work by Francis Vere (whom I believe is Catholic), in which he analyzes the basis of the Piltdown fraud quite closely and comes up with some amazing conclusions regarding Teilhard. I am enclosing a Xerox.

What I cannot understand is how a man with your generous spirit in the area of origins study can remain a member of the NABT Committee on Evolution Education, where men like Mayer, Moyer, and Steen continually exude an attitude of bigoted obscurantism that undermines their whole character as scientists. It would be advisable for them to change the name to the "Committee on Evolution Indoctrination."

With best personal regards,

George F. Howe

November 10, 1980

Dear Dr. Howe:

I am glad that you are enjoying *Viewpoints on Evolution and Religion*. I was sure that you would like Sylvia Clarence-Smith's article. She is a very brilliant young lady. I am sorry that she is not continuing in biology, but she has transferred to the Faculty of Education. While she will no doubt become an excellent teacher, I believe that she is quite capable of a good career at the university level. I think that James Henry's paper is the weakest in the collection, and I was undecided for some time whether I should include it. I finally decided in favor of it on the grounds that it represents a position which is rather widespread today: a generalized respect for his historical Christian background, without specific definition or commitment. I hope that I am not unjust to him in this evaluation. Finally, I hope that you read French with facility, for Laurent Labaky's essay is the best expression in the collection of a Catholic point of view, and the other papers in French are also interesting.

You are quite right that I am interested in Teilhard. I do not know Francis Vere, but I wonder if the paper you mentioned (but the Xerox was not enclosed) is related to one which was published by Stephen J. Gould in the August issue of *Natural History*. I wrote a reply to that article and sent it to *Natural History*. I have not yet heard from the editor. Possibly that journal publishes only papers by staff members of the American Museum of Natural History. I hope that this is not the case because, if so, it will be very difficult to publish my reply. Editors are quite naturally reluctant to publish anything which takes origin in a different journal. Just in case it is not published, I am enclosing a Xerox copy.

Now to the NABT Committee on Evolution Education. I do not personally know any of the other members. Moyer, as

President of NABT, published a letter in *BioScience* inviting
professionals in the study of evolution to volunteer for committee service. I responded. Later, it was announced that Mayer
would be the chairman. I have never met him, but he is well
known as the Director of BSCS [Biological Sciences Curriculum
Study] and I respect him for that. He wrote and asked if I would
agree to serve with him, and I did. He then asked me to suggest
other candidates. I submitted several names, none of which resulted in appointment. You mentioned Steen. I do not know him
but, like Moyer, he is not a member of the committee. In addition
to Mayer and myself, the other members are:

> Sidney Fox
> Jack Gerlovich
> Addison E. Lee
> Rev. Lazarus W. Macior
> John A. Moore
> Norman D. Newell
> Vera B. Remsberg

Of these, Fox, Moore, and Newell are scientists of outstanding
reputations, and I am happy to serve with them. I know little
or nothing about the others, and I will suspend judgment until
I have some basis for judgment.*

In writing to me about the potential work of the committee, Mayer said that "I believe that NABT should not operate
in a stimulus-response mode, but rather provide information
and help to teachers who wish better to understand the theory
of evolution and its consequences." I like that statement, and I
hope that the committee will generally work along those lines.
On the other hand, his letter to you was very harsh. He knows

---

* Editor's Note: The Reverend Macior, while working on the committee with
Dr. Dodson, reminded him that he had taught Macior at the University of
Notre Dame in the 1950s. Dr. Dodson and Dr. Howe later requested Dr.
Macior to write the Foreword for the correspondence published here because
of his conviction that "both creation and evolution are valid hypotheses in
different frames of reference."

that, for he wrote to the committee members: "You may think it an unusually harsh reply, but I have found that reasoned and rational answers have not turned away wrath . . . the time has come to take off the kid gloves . . . ." While I would have replied very differently, still he is chairman and I am not. And, if one disregards the angry rhetoric, his letter amounts to about the same thing as my letter to the editor of *BioScience*: debates do not count, but research published in professional journals does; and those who want to be taken seriously as scientists must follow the latter route.

Sincerely yours,

Edward O. Dodson

January 3, 1981

Dear Dr. Dodson:

Thanks for your kind response to my previous letter and for sending a Xerox copy of your response to Gould's article implicating Teilhard in the Piltdown hoax. I am sending you a copy of Vere as soon as it arrives, and three other works which speak to that same issue—one by the late and great W. R. Thompson of Canada; one by Rev. Patrick O'Connell, former missionary priest to China; and one by a Mr. Bowden of England. When all of these are mailed, I shall send a letter bringing up several points along that line.

I wish to write a second letter involving the exchange with Dr. Mayer of Colorado. Thanks for the details of the committee letter you shared with me. My second letter shall deal with that subject and its present status.

But the first letter is one in which we should come to grips with a few minor changes that you might consider in your letter to Gould, as well as the overall question of Teilhard's views and their implications for biology and theology.

May I suggest that, if you have any trouble at all getting your good letter published by *Natural History,* you change your plan and make the letter into an "article" in its own right. After you study the three or so sources I send you and do further research of your own, this reply of yours ought to make a very significant contribution. It is the first real defense of Teilhard I have read, concerning Piltdown. Most authors either implicate him directly or do so by innuendo. The article would be excellent.

More important than the question of whether or not Teilhard was implicated in the hoax are the ideas of Teilhard and the impact they have had on both biology and theology. My colleague Dr. John Meyer (an experimental physiologist, formerly

of the University of Louisville Medical College) recently prepared a term paper for a contemporary theology course. I enclose
a copy herewith for your analysis. As you point out, it is true
that Teilhard was not a trained theologian (any more than Darwin was a trained biologist). But Teilhard's writings have been
taken for THEOLOGY in both Protestant and Catholic circles, I
might add. And thus, we must carefully analyze the theological
implications of his books because of the impact they have had
on modern philosophy and theology of science.

On pages 1–2 of the paper, Meyer analyzes historical details that are certainly not new to you. But Meyer goes on in
later pages to deal with the issues Teilhard raised. For example,
on page 4, paragraph 2, Meyer (based on direct quotations from
Teilhard) asserts that Teilhard was a self-confessed pantheist.

Meyer holds that there is an inconsistency in Teilhard,
who held that evolution was orthogenetic (on the one hand) and
internally guided, but then saw man as being able to turn away
from or frustrate the whole process (p. 6, second from last paragraph).

Do you have comments regarding Meyer's conclusion on
page 9? I am sure John would be interested in your reactions
by way of reply, when and if you find the time.

Although I myself have made little or no study of Teilhard's life and am not very well versed on his scientific contri-
butions, I gave *The Phenomenon of Man* a rather careful reading
some years ago. As I read it, I was at the same time seeing rave
notices about the book from rather conservative Protestant theologians. Some of my friends at Westmont College were also
quite pleased with *The Phenomenon*. This brought to my mind
some major problems—how my scientific friends as well as religious ones could be at all excited about some of the problematic
themes I noted in Teilhard. Do you mind if I try a few of these
on you? I already know that you are a top scientist and a communicant Catholic and so it would be of interest to me to see
just how you square certain elements of Teilhard's thought with
your own religious and scientific tenets.

My overall criticism of the book is its dearth of real scientific subject matter. Did you sense in reading it that the good man produced reams of verbiage based on little evidence? In theology, for example, there are documents, arguments, and logical analyses on the one hand and there is the "hymn book" on the other hand. When I read *The Phenomenon*, it seemed to me that I was reading a "hymn book" of evolution which was beautifully written, inspiring, but seductively non-factual. It seemed to be a kind of mood music for evolutionists—a soft-sell job aimed at convincing people to believe something that would otherwise violate their common sense. I saw in *The Phenomenon* a lack of careful logic with emphasis on literary salesmanship. Perhaps you want an example. They are very numerous and one comes on page 35 in his "vision" (p. 36 of the Harper Torchbook edition): "In such a vision man is seen not as a static centre of the world—as he for long believed himself to be—but as the axis and leading shoot of evolution, which is something much finer." His whole section on the advent of life is fraught with praise but little fact. Throughout the book he usually assumed what was to be proved, just as the hymn book is of very little help to anyone looking for apologetic data. Thus, I could not understand why my scientist friends were so excited about the book.

The preceding would not be so much of a problem in Teilhard if he at the same time had recognized that he was merely spinning a thinly based philosophical web of factual nothingness; but it seemed at the same time he felt that it was tantamount to suicide (biologically) to believe otherwise than he: "But on the general and fundamental FACT that organic evolution exists, applicable equally to life as a whole or to any given living creature in particular, *all scientists are today in agreement* for the very good reason that they *couldn't practice science if they thought otherwise*" (p. 140, emphasis mine).

From this it would seem Teilhard was saying it is impossible to practise biology without evolution ideology. There are many medical, biological, physical, geological, and mathematical scientists who demonstrate by their lives and works in biology that Teilhard at this point was way off base.

Furthermore, throughout the whole of *The Phenomenon* Teilhard neglected to admit that there is a *theologically and scientifically* viable alternative to the views he was propounding. Can you excuse this failure on his part? "How could we hesitate even for a moment about the evolutionary origins of the layer of life on the earth?" (p. 138). When pressed for fossil data to support speculative theses, he stated: "What the antitransformists are demanding is nothing less than that we should show them the 'peduncle' of a phylum. But this demand is both pointless and unreasonable. To satisfy it we should have to change the very nature of the world and the conditions under which we perceive it" (p. 120). When pressed to show the linkers that thinking people might demand in support of transformist ideology, Teilhard offered nothing more than a vision: "By so doing, it separates them off and isolates them more and more in our vision, while at the same time, by another and more subtle process, it gives us the illusion of seeing them floating like clouds" (p. 120).

Modern scientific creationists would assert that this "rootlessness" to which Teilhard referred is evidence supporting DISCONTINUITY and rapid creative acts—something that Teilhard never discussed in his treatises. For example, on page 119 he ignores the possibility that gaps represent actual creative discontinuities: "As a result of this destruction, many gaps are continually forming in the ramifications of the animal and vegetable kingdom, and the farther back we go, the larger the gaps are . . . ." He goes as far as some evolutionists do today by implying that, if you don't buy his origins model, nothing can be understood: "I repeat this same thing like a refrain on every rung of the ladder that leads to man for, *if this thing is forgotten, nothing can be understood*" (p. 112, emphasis mine).

I realize that it can be easier and perhaps more satisfying simply to NEGLECT alternative viewpoints but I cannot and do not excuse my evolution-minded friends on this issue. Is there any excuse for failing to take alternatives seriously and deal with them rationally?

He continually begs the question he attempts to demonstrate—descent with modification as explaining ALL of life. For example, on page 107 he presents various "grades" of life in zoology but uses these as evidence for transformism when in fact these grades are FIXED and do not show evidence for the process he proposes.

In the face of the points I raise, how could Teilhard say on page 103 that his view of an evolving earth is " . . . a vision so homogenous and coherent that *its truth is irresistible*" (emphasis mine)? His next words are baldly true: "I provide no minor details and no arguments, but only a perspective that the reader may see and accept—or not see." Too bad he forgot about that openness later and asserted that science makes sense ONLY if you agree with Teilhard.

On page 98 he wrote in another context: "Fundamentally, is not everything apart from the present, mere 'conjecture'?"

Take his statement on page 99: "There is no lack of facts to support the idea that organized matter might have germinated periodically on the earth." I don't know what Teilhard was possibly thinking about by way of evidence when he wrote this. I periodically challenge evolution-minded friends (including Dr. Fox by private correspondence) to send me the repeatable, verifiable, "scientific" evidence that in fact life arose from non-life vast ages of time ago and *I have not received any valid answers.*

It is not wrong to use a hymn book and to sing the hymns as long as one in no way asserts that this hymn book is somehow an apologetic treatment of the Christian faith. Yet, in one sense, I judge this is exactly what Teilhard did. He wrote an evolutionary "hymn book" and then expected it to be taken as a strong apologetic. The bizarre outcome was that people *did* largely as he expected. But truth does not come by counting votes.

I want to close with one more proposition from *The Phenomenon* that never really seemed to square with the sacred Scriptures or Church doctrine. Let's quote Teilhard: "Man only progresses by slowly elaborating from age to age the essence and the totality of a universe deposited within him" (p. 180).

From this we conclude rightly that Teilhard believed man *arose* as an evolving group. However, in the book of Romans, chapter 5, verse 12, St. Paul wrote that it was "... through one man that sin entered into the world, and death through sin; and so death passed unto all men, for that all have sinned ...." In his writings, did Teilhard simply ignore the Fall? To do so would be theological catastrophe. Did he believe that a whole group of proto-hominids experienced the Fall together? St. Paul said that "one man" was involved—presumably the "Adam" of Genesis who together with his wife chose to disobey his Creator, later repenting. How did Teilhard envision the formation of the first man? Did the Creator form many "Adams" at once from a set of Sinanthropus ancestors? If so, what happens to the literal structure of Genesis 1–2 and the whole Bible, for that matter? An answer comes partially on page 159 where he wrote: "Because, right up to the Pliocene period, the primates remained the most 'primitive' of the mammals as regards their limbs, they remained also the most free. And what did they do with that freedom? They used it to lift themselves through successive upthrusts to the very frontiers of intelligence."

Would it be true to paraphrase this somewhat to say that man did not experience a creation in which he was at first "good" and then fell, but man AROSE? But if one takes this pull-yourself-up-by-your-own-bootstraps approach to origins and theology, then the whole topic of God reconciling Himself to us through Our Lord and Savior Jesus Christ makes little sense. "But God commendeth his own love towards us, in that while we were yet sinners, Christ died for us. Much more then, being now justified by his blood, shall we be saved from the wrath of God through him. For if, while we were enemies, we were reconciled to God through the death of his Son, much more, being reconciled, shall we be saved by his life and not only so, but we also rejoice in God through Our Lord Jesus Christ, through whom we have now received the reconciliation" (Romans 5, 8ff.).

If man has arisen, what happens to the Fall, the reconciliation of man to God by faith in Christ, and to personal salvation? If I arose from the brute, as Teilhard argued, and if then

I sin, there would be no need to "reconcile" me to the Holy Father because I am merely a stumbling product of an evolutionary heritage.

Thanks for writing,

George F. Howe

January 12, 1981

Dear Dr. Howe:

I have just received your letter of January 3. I am replying at once, although briefly, because the second semester is an extremely difficult one for me, and anything that is postponed is likely to be postponed for a very long time.

By now, you have probably received the note which I wrote to you at the beginning of the Christmas holidays. In the event that you did not, I will summarize. You sent me Vere's long paper under separate cover from the letter in which you mentioned that you were sending it, and it arrived just before the holidays. I said that I hoped to read it during the holidays, and in fact I did read it. Vere has brought together much evidence which suggests that there was a lot of incompetent work expended on Piltdown, and indeed the fact that the fraud remained undiscovered for so long supports this. I think, however, that Vere has also made a few mistakes of his own. In the Xeroxed paper which I sent you, I cited a book which I knew only from the review, *The Piltdown Men* by Millar. One of the readers of that paper very kindly sent me his personal copy of Millar's book, and I read that too during the holidays. I think that he did a better job than did Vere. He believes that G. E. Smith was the hoaxer and that Dawson was the first victim. He concedes, however, that only a confession could resolve the problem beyond doubt.

Also during the holidays, I studied the books of John C. Greene. You had asked whether I would like to reconsider my classification of him as a Protestant. I believe that he is, in fact, a Protestant, but he writes as an exceptionally objective historian of science, with minimal intrusion of his own position. Certainly, he could not be considered in any way a spokesman for any church. I listed the paper of Grabiner and Miller as "Miscellaneous." Perhaps it would be appropriate to include Greene in the same category. If I ever prepare another edition, I will give some thought to that question.

Finally, you raised many questions about Teilhard. It would take too long to write an adequate answer, but I agree with you on many points (but not all). I have a book manuscript on the subject. It will answer many of your questions if it ever gets into print. I have sent it to many editors without success. At present, an editor has had it since September, and I hope that that means that it is receiving thoughtful consideration, but I can only wait and see. Meanwhile, I am enclosing part of the preface, and this will suggest to you what are our areas of agreement and of disagreement. Perhaps this should cover also the paper of John Meyer; however, I will add a little more. In my preface, I pointed out that Teilhard is easily misunderstood, and I think that Meyer has fallen victim to that defect in Teilhard's writing. Just a few examples. In the first paragraph, he says that Teilhard collected various metal objects as a child, then worshipped them as idols. He was, indeed, a collector, and he did favor metal and stone objects, but there is no truth to that idol worship charge. Second, he says that the works of Teilhard were placed on the Index of Forbidden Books. This, again, is not true. Publication was forbidden by the Superior General of the Jesuit order, but unpublished works were never placed on the Index. When they were published after his death in 1955, they were not placed on the Index, and of course the Index as a whole was abolished by the Council. Finally, he quotes Henri de Lubac, who knew Teilhard well and has studied his works profoundly, but he does not seem to have gotten his message. de Lubac points out that the charge of pantheism against Teilhard is unfair and untrue. I think that Meyer was deceived by some unclear writing and probably by a bad translation too.

This is rather more than I set out to write. Again, thank you for your letter and for Meyer's paper, and especially for your suggestions regarding my Piltdown paper.

Sincerely yours,

Edward O. Dodson

January 23, 1981

Dear Dr. Howe:

This will be a rather brief letter, mainly to thank you for sending me Van Til's little book. I have not had time to read much of it yet, so I will reserve comment. My impressions are rather mixed at present, but they may be more uniform when I have read it all.

You may be amused, as I was, by an incident which happened in my general zoology class this week. I sometimes lead them in singing biological parodies of well-known songs. This week, I did it for the first time with this class. The song was "Down by the Old Lymph Stream." After class, one of the students came forward and asked if I had ever considered singing professionally. I replied that it was a little late for me to think of an alternative career, and that I sang very little music that was intended primarily for entertainment, as I sang mainly in church. He then said, "This is a church job. I am responsible for a large church choir, and we have paid singers to lead each section. Good tenors are hard to find, and I would like to hire you as our leading tenor." I then asked what church he represented, and he replied, "The Fourth Avenue Baptist Church." When I told him that I was singing for St. Paul's in the suburb in which I live, he assured me that the position would be available any time I might want it. Of course, I shall continue to serve St. Paul's, but it was nice to be asked, and I thought that the incident might interest you.

Duane Gish will be speaking on the campus next week, and I look forward to hearing him. He was here once before, but I was unable to hear him on that occasion because of a conflict of schedules.

Sincerely yours,

Edward O. Dodson

P.S. I was in error above. Dr. Gish will not be here. The first bulletin which I received simply announced that there would be a debate between Dr. Gish and Dr. Robinson of the University of Wisconsin. I have just seen a second, more detailed announcement. It says that this debate was taped at the University of Wisconsin, and that the video-tape will be shown here. I am disappointed, but I will go anyway.

February 10, 1981

Dear Dr. Dodson:

I too have fallen into considerable work this semester, so have delayed to this point in answering—but remember, this is how we handle our correspondence. If I don't hear from you for six months, that's all right—I do not thereby assume that the correspondence is over, but simply realize that you are very busy.

Now, it was nice of you to send that interesting report of how you were recruited for a Baptist choir. I have shared that with several folk here who all were amused and interested. At our own church—about three hundred members—we don't even pay the choir director, let alone the organist or the choir members.

Seriously, I would like the words sometime to "Down by the Old Lymph Stream" and some others you might have. This sounds like a fine exercise in fun and learning.

Your pages are fascinating and, as far as I am concerned, they correctly picture the work of Teilhard. I am enclosing a Xerox to show all the positive reactions I had here and there to what you had previously written. It is interesting that, while you and Simpson would be poles apart from me on origins philosophy, we all come up with the same analysis of Teilhard's statements (more or less independently). I certainly want to see the finished work.

I am enclosing several other items for your analysis as time permits—you may keep these, of course.

One is a piece written by the former head at the Zoology Department, University of Orange Free State—De Wit. He and I corresponded extensively. He wrote what I believe to be a balanced critique of Teilhard and evolutionism. The first thirty-nine pages deal with Teilhard and there is an extensive bibliography that also might interest you.

Another by someone you may have met or corresponded with—W. R. Thompson of Canada—also a Catholic. He wrote concerning Teilhard and in the process dealt with the evidence he felt implicated Teilhard in the Piltdown pageantry! I have specifically marked some of these passages.

A third is John Moore's review of the Thompson article. John has written you from time to time and has appreciated your cordial replies. Here, John was trying to bring Thompson to our readers because Thompson never really wanted to get very active in CRS.

Trust this all interests you. If nothing else, it simply supplies you with a few more pieces of literature that may or may not bear mention in your book and possible articles about Teilhard. I do trust you will consider writing a paper defending Teilhard at Piltdown. Your statements made sense to me and I would like to think that they would become part of the growing body of statements about that issue.

Best regards,

George F. Howe

March 7, 1981

Dear Dr. Dodson:

Thanks for the interesting book by O'Brien about testimonies of those who became Roman Catholics. I admire your interest in cabinet work. In your section, you correctly described the "modernistic" or "liberal" Protestant churches. My dad had an experience similar to that which you report—raised in a Methodist church (1903–1921) where book reports and social gospel were the order of the day. At age 33, he found in Scripture that he needed to make contact with God through Jesus—"I am the way, the truth, and the life; no man cometh to the father but by me." His mother was upset when dad told her he had received Christ as savior, saying, "Russell, you have *always* been a Christian." Thus it is assumed in some Protestant circles that all people who attend church or grow up in a Christian environment are "Christians," with no attention to *saving faith* and Bible doctrine.

Since you left Protestantism, interesting developments have taken place. "New wineskins" have been raised up by the Lord to contain the "new wine" of true Christian belief, including a whole group of independent alignment such as Regular Baptist, Orthodox Presbyterian, Free Methodist, and Pentecostal. These fundamental groups are generally alive and busy evangelizing the unsaved peoples of their own communities and the world at large. Even inside the historic churches whole segments have turned back to God, as in the "New Life" group of Methodists.

May I raise some friendly questions and offer some comments? Do Roman Catholic people sing hymns *to* the sacrament? Do they take such practice from Scripture directly or from church tradition?

It is correct to insist that the *practice* of Christianity be founded on doctrinal *principles* (p. 97). Certainly you are on Biblically solid ground to assert that the virgin birth of Jesus is *essential*!

Your stress on God the Father and Christ as His coeternal Son (p. 98) is valid. Sermons on secular subjects are still the bane of modernist churches, many of which are dying internally as a result.

It is sad that you encountered a stratified church system in which the poor felt ill at ease. This is frequently a weakness in Christian churches. I thank God that at our local church you will see shabbily clothed ex-alcoholics sitting next to and fellowshipping with millionaires. This should never change.

In your book I enjoy your stress on the Creator *apart* from the "created." Too bad Teilhard didn't read your book and apply it to his own *ramblings*.

On page 111 you assert that the Roman Catholic church has somehow avoided espousing "pet doctrines." Could the very concept of *venerating a wafer* as one means of salvation (grace) be considered a "pet doctrine" in context with Christ's and the apostles' clear words on how to be "saved" (John 3:16, 5:24, etc.)? Could a devout Roman Catholic possibly *miss* this critical issue entirely—placing his faith in communion bread rather than in a Risen Lord? How common would you suppose such a fatal misunderstanding could be among Roman Catholics at large? Could the very beauty of this spectacle cause some people to miss the whole core of Christianity and leave them trusting in a communion act, a gigantic church system, or even a wonderful Jewish girl instead of Jesus, the Risen Messiah, Son of God?

My own mother was confused at this very point. She had been a devout and faithful Roman Catholic, playing the organ for worship services (Mass, as you people call it). In it all she never realized her need to confess Christ as personal Lord and Savior (as in Romans 10:9–10). She did not know (as did the thief who died on the cross next to Christ) that she could be sure to be with Christ after death. Later, she saw these Bible truths clearly explained in an independent gospel church (not "Protestant" or "Catholic," but Biblical) and lived a devout Christian life with the *assurance of salvation* and the love of God in her heart.

In Miss Day's chapter, it is clear she came to Roman Catholicism but I could not put a finger on whether or not she saw Jesus as her personal savior. But Goldstein (pp. 150–151) seems to recognize that it is Christ who is the Way, the Truth, and the Life. If he believes this (really believes), God does not look for denominational labels, be they Roman Catholic or Baptist because, *if* Goldstein believes in Jesus as his Risen Lord and Redeemer, he thereby becomes a member of the only true "catholic" church—the body of all who are identified with God in Christ. Thus, it may surprise you to know that I recognize certain Roman Catholics *can be* and *are* saved insomuch as they came to God through the blood of Jesus. I expect to see all such people in heaven (Roman Catholics, Baptists, Lutherans, etc.). I am not a "Protestant" as I am not protesting against any particular Christian denomination. I am a "born again" Christian and am hence *brother* to *all* other true believers, no matter what their label.

I have been reading the other testimonies too and you can be sure I am evaluating them as the Bereans evaluated each new idea in apostolic times—by searching the Scriptures. I trust all this interests you and does not offend you, as I have not intended any offense.

Have you spent much time reading Karl Popper's assertions that evolution (macroevolution) "theory" is not a "scientific theory" but instead is a "metaphysical philosophy"? I enclose a paper for your files. I also enclose an abstract of a paper I have submitted for presentation at our local Southern California Academy of Science meetings in May. This is the "gospel" I am preaching to all my scientific colleagues: *"Believe* what you wish or what you feel most reasonable about *origins* but please don't call it *science!"*

Best personal regards. I shall send another book on Teilhard as soon as it arrives—it's presently on "back order."

George F. Howe

May 6, 1981

Dear Dr. Howe:

I have received several long letters from you since I last wrote. Now that an excessively busy semester is over, I will start catching up, but by means of a series of short letters rather than in one massive one. You asked some rather critical questions about my conversion, and you hoped that I would not be offended. I was not offended but, if I give adequate answers, you may feel that I am proselytizing. That is not my purpose at all. I assume that your choice is fully mature and that you will stand by it. I simply feel obliged to set the record straight, and I trust that this will not offend you.

It may be that you asked such critical questions because you thought that I was already proselytizing when I sent you O'Brien's *Where I Found Christ*. Again, that was not my idea at all. You had sent me Van Til's little book (incidentally, I think that he understands neither Teilhard nor Catholicism) and several other long papers, and I felt that it was appropriate that I give you a book. My choice was one which was very personally mine. Further, it answers a statement in one of your early letters to me: ". . . you are a theist, and will admit this—at least in private correspondence." The book establishes that my religious position is as much in the public record as is my scientific position.

After that introduction, it may not even apply to the balance of this letter, although it certainly will apply to my next one.

You cited Popper and asked if I were familiar with his works, and his apparent exclusion of evolutionary studies from the realm of science. The answer is a qualified "yes." I have come across Popper many times over the years, but I must admit that I aspire to considerably more knowledge of the philosophy of science than I can actually claim. While it is obvious that the study of any historical phenomenon differs in significant ways from the study of phenomena which can be repeated in the laboratory, similar reasoning might eliminate most of chemistry and physics, for no one has yet seen an atom or a molecule. Nonetheless, most of us have confidence in the findings of our friends in physics and chemistry, and a measure of verification may also be possible in evolutionary science. Popper was certainly using "metaphysical" in a sense radically different from its usual meaning in philosophy. Teachers of metaphysics would not find my book a useful class text. Further, did you see Russell-Hunter's letter to the editor of *Science* for April 17? He says that Popper has published a paper in *The New Scientist* in which he disassociates himself from the anti-evolutionary use of his philosophy of science. I have not seen that paper, but I intend to look it up, and you should too before you again quote Popper against the scientific character of evolutionary studies.

Well, there is a beginning, and I will try to continue in the near future.

Sincerely yours,

Edward O. Dodson

May 11, 1981

Dear Dr. Howe:

First, thank you for sending me Davidheiser's *The Quest of the Ctenophive*. I enjoyed reading it. If I were hunting ctenophives, I think that I would look on the parking lots of large office buildings just before the scheduled afternoon exodus. One might also hope for fair success near the coffee dispensers in mid-afternoon. I'm glad that you enjoyed my biological songs. In addition to the good fun which they provide, I find that they heighten student interest.

That leads naturally to choirs. That Baptist choir that tried to recruit me must be exceptionally well financed. Like yours, our English-speaking Catholic church has a strictly volunteer choir, including organist and director. Our French-speaking parish is larger and much longer established, and we have paid organist and director, both of whom are first-rate professional musicians. I sang with the English choir for fourteen years, but for the past ten years I have sung with the French choir.

As a prelude to some of your questions to which I referred in my last letter, let me say that my early background was probably rather similar to that of your father. Of the "new wineskins" which you mention—Regular Baptist, Orthodox Presbyterian, etc.—these, or their counterparts, were present at the time of my conversion, but they were less important than today, and they were generally regarded as "fringe groups."

Now, let me turn to your questions. First, "Do Roman Catholic people sing hymns *to* the sacrament? Do they take such practice from Scripture directly or from church tradition?" The balance of this letter will be concerned with these two closely related questions. The simplest answer to the first is simply "no." Catholics sing hymns to Christ, truly present in the Blessed

Sacrament. They sing in thanksgiving to Christ for His gift of Himself in the sacrament. Actually, as in many Protestant hymns, poetic license may result in misleading verses. We believe that He meant it quite literally when He said, "This *is* my body . . . ," not "This represents my body."

This interpretation is obviously scriptural, but it also has deep roots in tradition. I would like to discuss this further because it is often misunderstood by Protestants. I realize that you do not consider yourself to be protesting, and I congratulate you upon it. Nonetheless, the mere fact of centuries of separation makes for differences of interpretation which must be understood by reference to different frameworks of tradition—even if part of that may be a denial of the value of tradition. Protestants often think of tradition within the Catholic Church as being anti-scriptural teaching. On the contrary, Fr. Putz of Notre Dame likes to define tradition as the Church reading the Bible and meditating upon it. These are mutually supportive and corroborative sources of Christian truth, not competing or contradictory sources.

Nonetheless, there is more to it than that. The Gospel according to St. John ends with this verse: "But there are also many more things which Jesus did, which if they were written every one, the world itself (I think) would not contain the books to be written." Was all of that lost irretrievably? Do the majority of Our Lord's acts and words have no significance for our salvation? Or were they meaningful only for His contemporaries? And were they futile for us because they were not included in Scripture? I cannot accept the exclusions which these questions require if tradition be rejected. Further, Our Lord said, "He that heareth you, heareth Me; and he that rejecteth you, rejecteth Me; and he that rejecteth Me, rejecteth Him who sent Me." At the time that He spoke, the New Testament did not exist—not even one chapter—so that He had to be referring to an oral tradition of the apostles and their successors.

Similarly, St. Paul wrote (1 Cor. 11:2), "Now I praise you because in all things you are mindful of me, and hold fast the traditions, even as I delivered them to you." And again in 2 Tim. 2:1 and 2, "You, therefore, my son, be strengthened in the grace which is in Christ Jesus; and the things you heard from me in the presence of many witnesses, the same entrust to faithful men, such as will be able to teach others in turn." That is a good description of tradition, which complements and corroborates the Bible. These and other Biblical passages require tradition. That Protestants lost this supplementary source of Christian truth at the time of the Reformation is as serious a loss for them as would be the loss of several books of the Bible.

Another question, another letter.

Sincerely yours,

Edward O. Dodson

May 15, 1981

Dear Dr. Howe:

Let us continue now with installment three of this long "catch-up" letter. We are agreed that "It is correct to insist that the *practice* of Christianity be founded on doctrinal *principles* (p. 97)," referring to my article in *Where I Found Christ*. This is a necessary consequence of Our Lord's instruction to the apostles: " . . . teach them whatsoever things I have taught you." I am glad to learn that your own church, like ours, is well mixed socially and economically (i.e., not stratified).

You ask, "Could the very concept of *venerating a wafer* as one means of salvation (grace) be considered a 'pet doctrine' . . . ?" There are two major points here, and I will try to separate them. The first is indicated by the expression *"venerating a wafer"* (your emphasis). Your expression and emphasis seem to indicate that you regard the Bread of Heaven as simply a bit of pastry. There are few things more emphatic in the New Testament than that it is the true body of Christ. He said, "This is my body," and we believe that He meant it quite literally. Indeed, when He foretold that He would give His own body for their spiritual nourishment, many of his disciples said, "This is a hard saying," and they left Him. He could easily have kept them by telling them that He was only speaking figuratively. He let them go because He knew that they understood Him correctly and could not accept it. He suffered their loss rather than soften His "hard saying." Christ is not dissected, so He is present whole and entire in the Blessed Sacrament, and hence your depreciatory reference to a "wafer" indicates a misunderstanding which is very similar to that of the disciples who deserted Him because of this "hard saying."

The second aspect is the question of whether this is a "pet doctrine." In view of the repeated and emphatic statements

in the New Testament regarding the importance of the Holy
Eucharist, I would have to say, "no, unless you are prepared to
consider it a pet doctrine on the part of Our Lord." I refer you
to Mt. 26:26–29; Mk. 14:22–25; Lk. 22:19–20; Jn. 6:30–69 (a long
passage which treats other subjects but returns repeatedly to
the Eucharist); 1 Cor. 10:16–17; and 1 Cor. 11:23–32.

"Could a devout Roman Catholic possibly *miss* this critical issue entirely . . . ?" Human nature being what it is, certainly this could happen, just as devout Baptists may miss the
critical issue entirely. On the other hand, I would say that the
more devout the Catholic, the less probable this is. Our teaching
is very highly Christocentric, and the more devout the Catholic,
the more likely he is to be critically aware that the importance
of the Holy Eucharist derives entirely from the Real Presence
of Christ. And by the same token, are you altogether sure that
failure to appreciate this fact of New Testament revelation may
not lead astray some Baptists?

"Could the very beauty of this spectacle cause some people to miss the whole core of Christianity . . . ?" Again, human
nature being what it is, there is nothing that cannot be perverted nor that has not been perverted in some instances. But
surely Baptists are not unique in being immune to possibilities
of perversion. The good, the true, and the beautiful: these are
the traditional philosophical virtues, and they should all three
normally help to lead us to God. Is it not possible that some
Baptists (and other Protestants) lose their faith because they
find one of these pathways to God blocked or inadequately used
in their public worship? And when you speak of missing the core
of Christianity and instead "trusting in a communion act," you
simply make a mockery of New Testament doctrine and the
clear statement of Christ Himself: "Amen, amen [or, if you prefer, Verily, verily] I say to you, unless you eat the flesh of the
Son of Man, and drink his blood, you shall not have life in you.
He who eats my flesh and drinks my blood has life everlasting,
and I will raise him up on the last day. For my flesh is food
indeed, and my blood is drink indeed. He who eats my flesh and
drinks my blood abides in me and I in him. As the living Father

has sent me, and as I live because of the Father, so he who eats me, he also shall live because of me. This is the bread that has come down from heaven; not as your fathers ate the manna and died. He who eats this bread shall live forever" (Jn. 6:54–59).

It is not because of your devotion to the Bible, but in spite of it, that you play down the importance of the Holy Eucharist.

Well, this is quite enough—perhaps even a little too much—for one letter. I shall continue in the near future, and perhaps in one or two more letters I can complete this overly long sermon.

Let me add just one little item of news by way of explaining an enclosure. We have a mandatory retirement age, and I reached it last month. Accordingly, my retirement becomes effective on July 1. For several years, I have concluded my course in elementary zoology with a lecture in which I attempt to show that biology is not an isolated subject, but that it forms an important part of general culture. I illustrate it with a beautiful set of Kodachrome slides which I have accumulated over a period of many years. This lecture has always been received with some enthusiasm, but the students outdid themselves this year. They gave me a standing ovation which lasted more than five minutes. I was very deeply touched. Afterwards, several people asked for my text. Accordingly, I prepared it as carefully as I could and had a few copies Xeroxed. You will take sharp exception to some parts of it, but I think that it will interest you on the whole. Accordingly, I am enclosing a copy for you.

Incidentally, I expect retirement to be rather active. I have already arranged to teach part-time here in the fall, and I am going to investigate the possibility of teaching part-time some place down south during the winter semester. I will also continue to write.

Sincerely yours,

Edward O. Dodson

May 21, 1981

Dear Dr. Howe:

This should be the last letter of my "catch-up" series. Deo gratias! Quite naturally, your mother's experience has unique value for you, and this makes it difficult and somewhat distasteful for me to point out alternative interpretations. Nonetheless, let me say in all goodwill that, when I hear of someone leaving the Church, I always wonder if he or she was really devout and well informed. In some cases, I know that the person was not. One of the results of the Council was a general exodus of lukewarm Catholics. A good musician may play beautifully, but without conviction. Please remember that it was a Baptist church which tried to recruit me as a singer without asking what my religious convictions might be. As I mentioned in another context, all devout Catholics do have a sense of personal closeness to Christ. We do not generally use your phrase "personal savior," but neither does the New Testament, and a rose by any other name smells as sweet. As a Catholic, she should have known that all who love Our Lord and keep His commandments (Mt. 7:21), and who persevere (Mt. 10:22) in the faith to the end of their days, have His assurance of salvation (Rom. 11:22; Apoc. 2:10). This assurance is sealed and confirmed by the sacraments—all seven of them—which Christ gave to His Church to help His people along the road to salvation.

Why your mother did not see these things as a Catholic, I cannot say. It may be that the local clergy did not teach effectively, but it is unlikely that the fault was entirely on their side, for there were almost certainly true saints in the congregation with her—there usually are. Perhaps her practice of Catholicism had been like the practice of Judaism by those Jews whom Our Lord referred to as "uncircumcised of heart," although they practised the letter of the law. She is to be congratulated for finding these things which she should have found in the Church, but she paid a grievous price too. She lost the benefit of five and perhaps six of the sacraments, and she deprived you of your birthright. You may not be conscious of the loss, but that does not make it less real.

You refer to the "only true 'catholic' church—the body of all who are identified with God in Christ." The New Testament is replete with texts on the foundation, inspiration, and authority of the Church. Let us begin with Mt. 16:16–19: "And Simon Peter answered and said, 'Thou art the Christ, the Son of the Living God.' Then Jesus answered and said, 'Blessed art thou, Simon, Son of Jonah, for flesh and blood has not revealed this to thee, but my Father in heaven. And I say to thee, thou art Peter [i.e., Rock], and upon this rock [the Greek text says 'upon this same rock'] I will build my Church, and the gates of hell shall not prevail against it. And I will give to thee the keys of the kingdom of heaven: and whatsoever thou shalt bind on earth shall be bound in heaven, and whatsoever thou shalt loose on earth shall be loosed in heaven.'" One might also cite such texts as Lk. 24:49; Jn. 14:26; 1 Cor. 3:10–14; Eph. 2:20 and 5:32. For the importance of Peter (and his successors, even to John Paul II!), try Mt. 16:16–19; Lk. 5:3–11, 22:32; Jn. 21:15–19; Acts 5:15; 1 Cor. 15:5; and Gal. 1:18. Historically, for three-fourths of all Christian time, the Church of these passages was universally interpreted as the visible, historical Catholic Church, under the leadership of Peter and his successors. The Church has long acknowledged that many who are not formally its members are in fact spiritually part of it, because they truly love the Lord and want to keep His commandments, but because of accidents of history and education, they are separated from the "one fold and one shepherd." To paraphrase, the Church has for centuries taught that our separated brethren may achieve salvation, not because they are separated, but because they are truly members of the Church which, in many instances, they despise.

The true Catholic Church, then, is the visible Catholic Church of history, and you are probably a member of it in spite of yourself! Yet, your interpretation of these same passages is radically different. Why? Let me mention just two factors before this letter gets too long. First, English-speaking readers are often misled by a peculiarity of the English language. When Our Lord gave Simon a new name, Peter, He presumably spoke Aramaic, from which the word *Kephas* may be translated either as "Peter" or "rock." In Greek, the words are πετρος and πετρα, in Latin, *petrus* and *petra*, and in French, *Pierre* is the name, *la pierre* the common noun. Readers in most languages have generally agreed that it was Our Lord's intention to name Peter as the foundation rock of the Church. English-speaking Protestants have often been misled by the vagaries of their language, and some of them seem to feel that inspiration was given primarily to the translators of the King James version.

Second, you have suggested that doctrine is valid if it is Biblical, but not if it is traditional. Actually, there is not so simple a choice as that, for Biblical interpretation is inevitably influenced by the historical and cultural background of the interpreter, a complex of factors which is subsumed in tradition. The real choice is between different traditions. We draw upon a tradition which began with Christ, His apostles, and their successors, which was developed by the Fathers of the Church, and which has shown unbroken continuity of development even to our day. The other major tradition began with the reformers of the sixteenth century, is in some respects sharply discontinuous from historic Christianity, and includes elements designed to justify that discontinuity. Curiously, those of you who interpret the Bible on the basis of this latter tradition often don't even seem to realize that traditional factors enter into your interpretation of the sacred text. That doesn't change the fact. In fairness, I should add that many Protestant exegetes have developed an admirable degree of objectivity, and their works are used and honored in Catholic seminaries.

The prayer of Christ that "there shall be one fold and one shepherd" must be fulfilled. I confidently predict that in some future all sincere Christians will belong to one fold, and its earthly shepherd will be Peter's successor.

As a general commentary upon your questions, I suggest Mt. 7:3–5: "But why dost thou see the mote in thy brother's eye . . . ?" You hoped that I would not be offended by your barrage of rather critical questions. I was not offended, but I could not answer adequately without being rather blunt. I hope that this has not offended you.

Sincerely yours,

Edward O. Dodson

June 30, 1981

Dear Dr. Dodson:

Now my turn to catch up has come. Thanks for the series of letters and Xeroxes. Congratulations on the well-deserved acceptance your speech on Seven Pillars received and on your retirement. I trust the years ahead will be satisfying and productive.

In Seven Pillars I enjoyed the two references to the Creator, your emphasis on the vibrant quality of cave art, and your awe for natural phenomena—desiring to bring the spirit of liberal arts back to biology. As you guessed, I take issue with the idea that homology " . . . must be based upon inheritance from a common ancestor" when in fact it may mean common design features incorporated in unrelated organisms (carburetors in trucks or motorcycles, for example). I would point to Linnaeus and Pasteur rather than Darwin as developing the real unifying principles that brought order to post-Renaissance biology—Linnaeus developing the fabric of taxonomy with which we still clothe ourselves and Pasteur having finally put to bed the idea of spontaneous abiogenesis which inhibited earlier biology and still dogs our efforts in terms of the Urey–Miller nonsense.

Regarding the Gould publications, I have benefitted much from the whole exposé. It is unfortunate that you didn't have proofreading privileges with the letter but I guess editors seldom do for letters. Two of the writers each agreed that the key question is why so many otherwise notable scientists fell for the hoax. I believe they had an unwholesome eagerness to find confirmatory evidence for their own origins belief that man and ape have come from common ancestry. Herein also lies a lesson for all of us origins people today—not to get unreasonably eager about one particular data item but to build a large case not dependent on one or two fragmentary pieces of evidence.

Washburn must not rule out the possibility of a joke. Many people go to great lengths to perpetrate jokes (during and after college days). Washburn and von Koenigswald were both unduly hostile in their critiques of Gould but it matters not because Gould manifested a biased attitude, using slanted phrases and clever statements rather than dealing with concrete issues throughout. Gould's main thrust that a volume of evidence pieced together points toward Teilhard is his main contribution. I sent Gould a copy of Vere's book that I sent to you earlier. Perhaps it will interest him. However, it seemed that you and the others were able to answer these various links with seemingly credible alternatives. The spirit of your letter was wholesome, as has been the tenor of all your letters to me— attributable, I believe, to the fact that you revere the Christ who alone can bring charity to the hearts of men in the midst of a contest. The section beginning "After all of this, I must concede that it is possible that Gould is right . . ." evidenced your desire to see all sides. I believe the greatest contribution you made in the exchange was to show that Sollas might have been the accomplice rather than Teilhard.

Perhaps now would be the time for someone to take all the arguments, list them, explore their bases briefly, and then summarize. We can conclude, I believe, that there are several people who are possible accomplices, any one or more of whom may be implicated or absolutely innocent—Sollas, Smith, and Teilhard. Even Dawson may have been "set up" by someone else, as Vere argued. My original idea that Teilhard WAS the man is shattered by the fact that others had access to bones and actually purchased dye! I have come to the conclusion personally that I cannot possibly say right now with the evidence that is available who is involved and who is innocent.

In your letter of May 6 concerning Popper's assertions that macroevolution fails the philosophical tests of "science," you asked or rather asserted that, if we used the same criteria, we would be required to "eliminate most of chemistry and physics, for no one has yet seen an atom or a molecule . . . ." Not so. Chemistry and physics (even though highly theoretical) stand

Popper's tests. In both cases it is possible to make predictions, devise experiments, and either support or falsify the theories. It's not a matter of being able to see or not to see an atom; it's a matter of whether or not we can devise experiments bearing on atoms. So far, most of the evidence has been in support of the atomic theories but, should some bright young physicists or chemists devise new experiments that would show otherwise, we would either modify or abandon our present ideas, if we are scientists. Not so with macroevolution—no crucial experiments can be performed and it is thus "safe" from any scrutiny by such scientific probes.

At the possibility of repeating myself too much, I must remind you that we ought to distinguish carefully between this and MICROevolution which in several instances can be tested and therefore is "scientific" (change in gene frequencies for color in British moths and a new group of rabbits on the island of Porto Santo that don't breed with mainland rabbits, as examples). When you wrote that "verification may also be possible in evolutionary science," you are correct only insofar as you speak about MICROevolution. As Gould has pointed out, the real problems of speciation and origin of higher taxa (MACROevolution) do not submit to neo-Darwinian methodology. The really big matters are without support and cannot be examined by scientific procedures and therefore Popper's criteria demonstrate that macroevolution (like scientific creationism) is outside science. This does not mean that a macroevolutionist never deals with scientific evidence. In fact both he and his scientific creation colleagues spend most of their time thinking about how their model fits or doesn't fit with the data of the natural sciences. But the real issue of never being able to test the results applies equally to both origins models.

It is too bad that Popper's academic colleagues drove him to recanting his earlier clear expressions of truth—an example of sheer harassment. What he could have said and should have said in answering these bad-tempered evolutionists is that to say macroevolution is "outside science" is not to make an anti-evolutionary statement. If I say "macroevolution is outside science" or "macroevolution is not a scientific theory" I have not criticized the model at all; I have merely made a true statement about its philosophical status. The model can still be debated and judged worthy or less than worthy by other criteria. Evolutionists weaken their own case with logical people when they attempt to assert that macroevolutionary phenomena are part of "science." So perhaps I should simply keep quiet and let them keep on doing that, as it is so philosophically naive that in itself it will work against the acceptance of macroevolutionary models.

By the way, all of this is not just some batch of ideas that Popper alone defends. Please find enclosed a set of statements by many workers regarding their own admission that macroevolution should not be forwarded as a "scientific" theory.

Thanks again for the book *Where I Found Christ*. You may certainly relax (regarding comments in the May 6 letter)—the thought never crossed my mind in reading the material that you were attempting to proselytize and, even if you had been, I would have enjoyed it as I appreciate frank discussion of spiritual matters with others. I understood that you sent it to show your theistic Catholic stance was as much part of the "public record" as are your works in genetics. This is the way all biologists who delve into philosophical issues should operate. Every person has a theological root from which he works and some, like you and me, take an above-board approach by letting the public know our stance. Others, whose names I shall not mention, try to pose as neutral or a-religious when in fact their commitment is just as much religious as is our own.

I am pleased to learn the surface reading of those testimonies is false and that Catholics actually sing to Christ, not the sacrament. I am also interested to learn you equate John 21:25 in part with apostolic and post-apostolic traditions (a reading of the passage which may or may not have been the prophetic intent of Christ's words through John).

Your citation of Luke 10:16—"He that heareth you, heareth me; and he that despiseth you, despiseth me; and he that despiseth me, despiseth him that sent me"—had an immediate and direct reference to the seventy disciples who were going out on a mission to tell people in nearby towns that the Kingdom of God had come. If it has application to the Church which came some years later, that application would be more general and would apply to each believer, as Peter himself told us we are all priests (see 1 Peter 2:5).

In one of your letters you indicated that those who left Rome originally or at other points in time were people who completely threw out the tradition. Actually, when Christians left one church or another to start new groups, they did so generally attempting to restore Christian practice to a tradition which more closely approximated the texts of Scripture and the patterns of the early Church. In a sense they were seeking for a return to the true pattern—not throwing over tradition entirely, but revising it as they were led (I believe) by the same Spirit that Peter recognized as the one which indwells every true believer.

Your words regarding the "bread of heaven" were both interesting and clear. It is good that we view this bread in such a light that the chance is minimized for someone to miss the Christ and pay homage to the pastry. If that never happens to Catholics or if it does not happen on a widespread basis, fine. It is possible, as you suggested, that Baptists too may place faith in this same ordinance or in some other ordinance rather than in the Risen Lord.

In John 6, we have a passage where Christ was speaking figuratively to His critics (the Jewish leaders). He made it clear that people must partake of Him. Did these words have reference to the ordinance of communion which had not yet been established? Dr. Dodson (and I suppose most Catholics) would say "yes." I and many others would say "no" because in John 6:47–48 Our Lord told the same people " . . . he that believeth on me hath everlasting life. I am that bread of life." Christ spoke here about *believing* in Him as the means of grace and the Last Supper hadn't even taken place yet. Therefore, "eating of that bread" (verse 50) which you quoted surely means a spiritual feast in which the sin-sick soul turns to Christ as Lord. In Mt. 26, Mk. 14, and Lk. 14 we also find that the bread and cup are posted as figures to remind true believers periodically of their total faith in Christ.

Hebrews 10 presents the interesting message to believers about the finished nature of Christ's work. The Hebrews' writer here was obviously speaking to Jewish believers, some of whom may have had the tendency to desire that all new Christians in general and certainly they themselves in particular should abide by the rituals and ordinances of the Jewish faith. But we are told that these legalistic sacrifices offered "year by year" or "continually" can never make the bearers perfect, "For it is not possible that the blood of bulls and of goats should take away sins" (verse 4). See verse 11: "And every priest standeth daily ministering and offering oftentimes the same sacrifices, which can never take away sins: But this man, after he had offered one sacrifice for sins for ever, sat down on the right hand of God . . . ," and verse 14: "For by one offering he hath perfected for ever them that are sanctified." Note the same idea in verses 16–18: "This is the covenant that I will make with them after those days, saith the Lord, I will put my laws into their hearts, and in their minds will I write them; And their sins and iniquities will I remember no more. Now where remission of these is, there is no more offering for sin." Amazing words.

I agree with John O'Brien (out of context!) when he wrote that finding Christ is by "the mysterious workings of divine grace upon the human soul." The true Church which you see as Rome and which you foresee as becoming "one fold, and its earthly shepherd will be Peter's successor" (May 21) already is ONE and is already consummated without any need of or help from the Pope. It is composed of all those who receive that grace that O'Brien brought up and it has nothing to do with denominational labels or church officials. Now you are quite right to say that someone never need use the phrase "personal savior" to be in proper relationship with Christ. Your view of the Roman Catholic position regarding "separated brethren" was most interesting and informative. By the same token, my prayer for Catholic people everywhere is that their own ritual will not cloud for them the real meaning of what it is to be born again—

a statement that IS in the Bible. You feel that possibly I am safe "in spite of myself" and I take the same view of Catholics who truly seek out that living bread which is the living Christ—those whom He judges as truly being born again of faith. Based on what is found in Scripture, one can be reasonably certain that God will accept such people on the basis of their pure faith in the Redeemer, despite whatever other unscriptural trappings they embrace. Have we found a common denominator right here??? If not, I have enjoyed the exchange of ideas and never really looked at it as proselytizing either way. I believe one should promote the concept of being born again first and foremost.

I have been having a productive time this summer. I have written an origins paper based on research I published last year in SCAS [Southern California Academy of Sciences]. In a short comment after a talk at the SCAS meetings, one speaker put me on to a place near here which is one of the five last remaining stands of a native California species of grass—*Stipa pulchra*. Although not yet a "vanishing species," it now obviously has only very limited distribution, whereas it originally covered large sections of the California valleys. Once each week I go to Hungry Valley to undertake a baseline study of the area for myself and others who may later wish to see if it is shrinking or stabilized at this spot. Perhaps I can likewise come up with some reasonable suggestions to the B.L.M. [Bureau of Land Management] about fencing off and preserving certain tracts; in fact I believe they already have such plans.

Other projects have included rewriting a manuscript that one society rejected about nine months ago and sending it as a "brief note" to another. It was too long in the first place for the data I had. I believe the germ of what I have found, however, is publishable—ten years of observations in our chaparral forest showing that chamise shrubs (our little resprouting "fire-balls" on the hillsides) can actually be killed by herbivores AFTER they have survived the intensity of fire. No mention of this phenomenon is in the literature that I can find.

My colleague Meyer has resigned and a man named Dennis Englin (presently in Billings, Montana) is returning to our faculty as Meyer's replacement. Dennis taught here for nine years, left us for four years, and really jumped at the chance to return. The dearth of jobs in academic fields right now is appalling. I have an excellent former student who earned the M.S. degree in plant taxonomy last year from Northern Arizona University, Flagstaff. He wrote a hundred-page dissertation on the vegetation of one particular Arizona valley. Presently he is teaching high school and dissatisfied. If things get much worse we'll have to encourage our better students to take vows of POVERTY as the Catholic priests do.

Here's wishing you a fine summer. Sorry to make the letter so long but I had the time to answer your four epistles, so I decided to go for it. I value our correspondence and always welcome your letters and/or reprints when and if time permits.

Sincerely,

George Howe

August 31, 1981

Dear Dr. Howe:

I would like to clear up a couple of things which remain from before our postal strike. It seems as though we were incommunicado for most of the summer. You may remember that you sent me a copy of the abstract of a paper in which you summarized your case against evolution. I think that it was a California Academy of Sciences paper. I reprinted your abstract on my final examination in my course on evolution, and I asked for a commentary upon it. This was one of several topics among which students could choose. I am enclosing a copy of the best essay which I received. Unfortunately, the student, Carole Dignard, wrote in French. I'm sure that you can read French, although, if you are a typical American, you will have to work pretty hard to do it.

Second, I looked over my letter of May 15, and I saw that I had left out an important part of the answer to one of your questions, that of whether the doctrine of the Eucharist is a pet doctrine in the Catholic Church. What I tried to show, I hope successfully, is that this is a valid doctrine upon which Christ Himself placed great emphasis. Yet it is quite possible for a pet doctrine to be valid and important. It is not invalidity that makes it a pet doctrine; rather, it is the tendency to emphasize it to a degree which eclipses other doctrines of importance. Catholics, like everyone else, may have a tendency to go off balance, but the Church continually calls them back by insisting upon the importance of the rest of the deposit of faith, for example, all of the articles of the Apostles' and Nicaean creeds. Thus, there is continual pressure against the development of pet doctrines.

Sincerely yours,

Edward O. Dodson

October 9, 1981

Dear Dr. Dodson:

Thanks for a final copy of your treatise on Teilhard. The more I look at this, the more I believe it might interest our CRS readers. If perchance you wished to send it to Harold Armstrong in Kingston, Ontario, Canada, he might just be interested in the material. If you have other plans for it, well and good.

I haven't gotten the student's article in French translated yet. I took two years of French in high school but promptly forgot a good deal of it because I took five years of Spanish and two of German. I used Spanish and German as my two languages for the Ph.D. at Ohio and have never really gone back to revamp my French. I have a friend who will help me as soon as he returns from travels in Washington state.

I also enjoyed the little Frank and Ernest cartoon! They are always funny. We both know from the Bible, however, that even if God created, we need not blame *Him* for evil things. No need to bring in evolution as a way to "save face" for God. All we need do is take Satan and the Fall very literally and we'll find the root of all evil (both biological and spiritual)—evil which tainted an otherwise *good* creation. I think we technicians in the sciences have probably done lots of harm by turning people away from the reality of a spiritual world—principalities and powers as the Bible says (spiritual wickedness in high places). To someone who takes evil and Satan literally, there's absolutely no need to use evolution as an "escape valve" to help us keep from blaming God for biological evil. Actually, I almost hesitate to write about all this, because you probably agree *and* you probably laughed at Frank and Ernest without putting any stock in their faulty philosophy.

I always enjoy your letters and find them a refreshing change from those of Dr. Edwin Steen, who calls me a "quack," a "charlatan," etc.!! Also, there are several other evolutionists who simply have *stopped* corresponding with me because it is evidently beneath their professional dignity to dialogue with a dirty creationist biologist! In your letters and from a few (very few) other evolutionists, I have noted the respect of a colleague who disagrees but understands and even appreciates the arguments of an alternative view.

Best regards, and I trust you are enjoying your new status,

George F. Howe

October 16, 1981

Dear Dr. Howe:

I received your letter of June 30 about two months late because of our postal strike. I hope that that issue will remain settled far into the future, but that is an exceedingly militant union. Thank you for the many Xeroxed papers and portions of books which you sent, among others a paper by Gould in *Paleobiology* and letters to the editor of *Nature*, including one from Gould. I have to ask whether this man knows his own mind. On page 126 of the *Paleobiology* paper, he says, "I believe that essentially all macroevolution is cladogenesis," yet, in his letter to the editor of *Nature*, he says, "I am not a cladist." Regarding the Piltdown fraud, I agree with you that the available data simply do not permit a decision on who the conspirators may have been. By the way, the Xerox Corporation should elect you to its Board of Directors. You are one of the mainstays of their prosperity!

You say that "It is too bad that Popper's academic colleagues drove him to recanting his earlier clear expressions of truth—an example of sheer harassment." Academic harassment can be very real, as I well know. My old friend and mentor, Richard Goldschmidt, suffered much abuse because of his rejection of the neo-Darwinian synthesis, and I have taken some flak myself because I have presented Goldschmidt's views sympathetically. Nonetheless, I am not aware that Popper has suffered any such harassment. You yourself sent me numerous quotations from academics who quoted him with approval. I think that Popper simply reacted against the use of his ideas in support of special creation. He had (deliberately?) overstated his case against evolutionary science, and now he has acted to remove a misunderstanding of his position.

I agree that there are important differences between *micro*- and *macro*evolution, and that microevolution is much more securely established than is macroevolution. I don't believe, however, that the barrier between them is so imposing as you suggest. Many aspects of macroevolution are falsifiable. As my student, Carole Dignard, wrote in a paper which I sent you, demonstration of random distribution of fossils in time would falsify evolution (macro-). For that matter, the whole of macroevolution would be falsified if it were demonstrated that the earth were a recent creation. That is, macroevolution requires long periods of time and, if they were not available, there could have been no macroevolution. It would be falsified if the cytochrome c data showed closely similar sequences in taxonomically widely separated groups and widely different sequences in closely related groups. It would be falsified if there were confusion of homology and analogy in the series of comparative anatomy. Orthogenesis has been falsified by the data of the fossil record. Collectively, these and other available examples negate your statement that "it is thus 'safe' from any scrutiny by such scientific probes." I agree that some of these evidences are understandable under the hypothesis of special creation as well as that of evolution, but that still leaves evolution a viable hypothesis. So the case is not so different from physics and chemistry as you say. You say that in the latter sciences, it is possible "to make predictions, devise experiments, and either support or falsify the theories." Certainly, "prediction" of the past is contradictory but, as indicated above, data may potentially falsify macroevolution, and some macroevolutionary hypotheses have been falsified.

By the way, as you are interested in the Gould–Eldredge idea of punctuated equilibrium as evidence of lack of applicability of the concepts of microevolution to macroevolution, you should read the following current papers:

Cronin, J. E., N. T. Boas, C. B. Stringer, and Y. Rak. 1981. "Tempo and mode in hominid evolution." *Nature* 292: 113–122.

Stebbins, G. L., and F. J. Ayala. 1981. "Is a new evolutionary synthesis necessary?" *Science* 213: 967–971.

When you say that "The really big matters are without support . . . ," I agree with you, but on a somewhat different basis than you had in mind. As indicated above, I believe that there is real support for macroevolution, although it leaves a lot to be desired. Several years ago, I had a student who was profoundly disturbed by his studies in biology. "We don't even know what life is," he complained, "yet we are asking all kinds of questions about little aspects of it." I told him that, in the history of science, it was long ago found that little progress was made as long as attention was focused on the big questions. But when these were broken down into a series of little questions, then it became possible to devise experiments which would clarify various aspects. And when a lot of little problems have been solved, they may collectively begin to make the larger questions intelligible. An overall attack on the problem of macroevolution probably is not possible, but many small parts of it have been successfully attacked. If we compare it to a jigsaw puzzle, then controversies like the present one indicate that the solved area of the puzzle is not sufficiently large to clarify the broad picture, but I think that there are enough pieces in place to confirm that there is a picture—a macroevolutionary picture. One may hope that future research will clarify at least the major features of that picture.

You suggest that Luke 10:16 applied only to the seventy disciples. It certainly had a very immediate application to them. Perhaps there are some things in the New Testament which applied only to the immediate situation described, but generally they are there because they have significance for the Christian community until the end of time. This passage should be read in relation to the many other passages which refer to the commission given to the Church.

You question the applicability of John 6 to the Eucharist on the grounds that the sacrament had not yet been established. Of course, it had not been established, for this occurred only at the Last Supper. Our Lord, however, was well aware of His intention to establish it, and He spoke prophetically, as in so many other passages. Outside of the concept of Holy Communion, His metaphor would have to be considered a rather strange one. Further, He suffered the loss of many disciples who found it a hard saying that they must eat His flesh and drink His blood. It would have been so easy to reclaim them by some such statement as "He that believes in Me shares my life and has everlasting life, and it is only in this figurative sense that you must partake of My body and blood." There is no such passage. He let them go because He knew that they understood Him correctly, and He suffered their loss rather than explain away the importance of the sacrament of His body and blood. But even under your interpretation, it would seem to me to be unnecessary to minimize the value of the sacrament.

The first Christians did, of course, regard themselves as faithful Jews, Jews for whom the Old Testament had been fulfilled, Jews for whom the sacrifices of the Old Law had been replaced by the perfect sacrifice of Christ. They anticipated the transition of Judaism as a whole to its perfect form, which is Christianity. Unfortunately, this was not to be, at least until a distant future.

Peter, in 1 Pet. 2:5, is not saying that every Christian is a priest. In part, he is contrasting Christians under the new dispensation with Jews under the old. Only Levites could be priests (i.e., empowered to offer sacrifice). Under the new dispensation, any man may become a priest. But further, we all participate with the priest in offering the sacrifice of the Mass, which is the unbloody repetition or continuation of the sacrifice on Calvary. Thus, we all share in the priestly function. Similarly, in verse 9, he is not saying that we all are royalty; rather, he is using the metaphor of the time to express great importance. Also, the Christian who shares the sacrifice of Christ also shares something of His royal destiny. As we sing, "Je suis mendiant, mais fils du roi"—"I am a beggar, yet the son of the King."

I agree with you that God does not need a Pope. Neither does He need any Baptist minister. Indeed, He does not need mankind, not even—suffer the thought—Ed Dodson or George Howe. God is wholly self-sufficient. In His mercy and love, however, He chose to create us and, when we fell from grace, He chose to redeem us by the blood of His only Son. In His mercy, He chose to establish His Church upon the rock which was Peter, and He gave to Peter and to all of his successors the keys of the Kingdom. It was Our Lord's clearly expressed intention that Peter and his successors should direct His Church and administer His sacraments. Therefore, *we* need the Pope even though God needs no man whatever.

In conclusion, I agree that we have found common ground. We both recognize that the other has the means of salvation. I'm sure that we have much more common ground than that for, although our correspondence has centered on our differences, we worship the same Holy Trinity, and we are undoubtedly agreed on many articles of faith, as expressed, for example, in the Apostles' and Nicene creeds.

I'm glad to learn that you have had so productive a summer. I'm particularly pleased to learn about your work with *Stipa pulchra*, as species like this, whose habitat is rapidly shrinking, present an opportunity which may not be available for long. Also, such studies may contribute to their conservation. I'm also pleased to learn about your long-continued study of the chaparral. Publication of such work in good, refereed journals is the key to earning scientific credibility, and it is the real answer to people like Steen (your letter of October 9 has just arrived). Yes, I too laughed at the Frank and Ernest cartoon without taking it seriously. I appreciate your problem in reading French. I took two years of Spanish and, when I went to Spain, I would have been lost without my phrase book. Those undergraduate years are a long way back, and there is no way to maintain linguistic competence without using the language. Of course, I speak French every day.

Sincerely yours,

Edward O. Dodson

Undated (probably Spring 1982)

Dear Dr. Dodson:

It has taken altogether too long to answer your letter of October 16! But it is perhaps well that I have been so delinquent because I have found in the interim a book you will surely want to read: *Evolution from Space* by Fred Hoyle and Wickramasinghe. This is a tightly reasoned treatise in which the authors assert that there are severe and insurmountable problems in megaevolution. For example, they take the very cytochrome c data that you and other megaevolutionists cite as support for overall relatedness and they turn them *against* the mega view. On pages 19–20 they take data from hemoglobin in legumes to show that the mega model is not what it purports to be. On other pages they ask how evolution can be assumed to have produced vision in *Drosophila* involving 2537 Å when these flies are not and have never been exposed to 2537 Å to allow selection for or against mechanisms that will permit the origin of the capacity for such sight. On and on they deal with biochemistry, fossils, and other fields.

In the October 16 letter you ask for falsifiable aspects of megaevolution and in fact you even show how it could be falsified but has not. Actually, this book contains the data and interpretation that you would need to close the books on megaevolution as already falsified. But I do not cherish any hopes at this point that you or other megaevolutionist friends will change your positions one iota based on Hoyle's work. He says that people (megaevolutionist people) are willing to settle for weak explanations because of obvious sociological pressures to affirm some type of evolution.

I can only hope that you will *read* this book. There are many reasons why you and people of your view and position will neglect to do so. You are in a position of security within the

scientific community. This depends not only on the character of
your scientific accomplishments but also on the fact that you
adopt and champion the most popular origins model. Furthermore, you have probably spent considerable time trying to point
out to Catholics and other Christians that it is possible to have
their "cake" (orthodox Christianity) while they eat it too (megaevolution). While both of these phenomena may be quite personally satisfying to you, they have little or nothing to do with
the falsity or validity of the actual origins questions involved—
as I am sure you realize. Thus, I hope I can jar you loose from
what must be a most enviable feeling of inner complacency at
this point in your most productive career. I have deeply appreciated the warmth and cordiality you have shown to me but I
must come back strongly to the things I have said in earlier
letters: (1) creationists do perform valuable research but they
experience a "closed-door" policy from peer review editors—a
policy that you do not even believe exists; (2) the overall megaevolution view looks solid and is so, but this depends largely on
the skill with which media people like Abelson, Mayer, Moyer,
and others, together with the help of the ACLU [American Civil
Liberties Union], have thus far successfully convinced judges
and others that instruction regarding the scientifically based
creation model should be suppressed in public school classrooms;
(3) megaevolutionism enjoyed a preferential (although, I trust,
short-lived) status in scientific circles because powerful critical
volumes such as those of Hoyle, Macbeth, and Kerkut have
largely been ignored.

I deeply enjoyed the theological discourse you presented
in your last letter too. I certainly have enlarged my understanding of the Roman Catholic mind as a result of your generous
sharing. You have probably come to realize, likewise, that media
hucksters have distorted the position of the so-called evangelical
Christian beyond recognition! In fact, we hold to the same pure
gospel that a Bible-oriented Catholic would embrace—there
being, of course, differences on matters here and there, as we
have discussed.

And when it comes to your own seeming reticence to evaluate and to promulgate the weaknesses of the mega model, I can understand all of that in light of the vested interest you surely have at this point in your career with a model (be it ever so bad) that you have promulgated, defended, and promoted. It is just a bit sad, however, that you cannot be motivated in spite of all this to seek out the critique of the view, rather than trying to sell the idea that the big picture is pretty much in place. It is sad because you could be sure this other way that you were helping students and others to see both sides of a controversial issue, no matter what you have found to be most satisfying from a psychological and philosophical standpoint. The matter of truth must override established preferences or even gut feelings that many have regarding the authenticity of evolution.

Thanks again for listening and I trust retirement (and I'm sure you're not really retired) has brought you great satisfaction thus far.

Your friend,

George F. Howe

P.S. Yes, I have read and appreciated the writings of Gould and Co.!! But, although we as creationists deeply enjoy Gould, he hates our guts because he is more radically committed to the overall "faith" of evolution than any of my Christian brothers, like you, *and* understandably so when you consider his politics (Marxism) and his own religion (atheism).

April 14, 1982

Dear Dr. Howe:

Thank you for your recent letter (undated), and for the several reprints of your new column, "From the Desk of Dr. George Howe." It arrived while I was on an extended trip out of town. I am only gradually catching up. No, I have not yet seen the new book by Hoyle and Wickramasinghe, but I intend to read it. I have read some reviews. The general viewpoint of the reviewers is that these men are superb in astronomy, cosmology, and mathematics, but that their lack of familiarity with biology leads them astray in the present book. I will form my own judgment when I read the book. Meanwhile, let me point out that their viewpoint is not much more congenial to yours than to mine. They see the germs of life as coming to earth from outer space, but that requires a lot of evolution after they get here. And they require a lot of time, as Wickramasinghe stated so bluntly at Little Rock.

You say that "creationists do perform valuable research but they experience a 'closed-door' policy from peer review editors." I know that creationists can publish in the standard biological journals. My friend and colleague, Vadim D. Vladykov, a life-long creationist, is one of the most respected ichthyologists in the world, and his publication list is a long one indeed. When he speaks his mind on evolution and creation, he gets a respectful hearing, if not agreement, because his colleagues know that he speaks on the basis of profound research on the fishes which he studies. Again, E. Norbert Smith is a very active young creationist who is currently publishing good research in physiology (animal). He is working toward status similar to Vladykov's, and he is likely to achieve it because his colleagues know that he is publishing sound physiology. I would like to see you publish your research in physiological ecology, and I am confident that you could publish it if you would write as you did when you published your doctoral thesis, presenting the data and the necessary conclusions, but avoiding conclusions which go far beyond the data (i.e., not claiming that this establishes creationism). You could, however, point out that the data are not readily interpretable in terms of this or that aspect of evolutionary theory, and the more specific you make this point, the better will be your chances of publishing it. Then, after you have published a considerable series of such papers, you could publish a review, bringing all of these results together, along with other related investigations, and you could say that these many evidences collectively require you to reject evolution in favor of creationism. If you had published twenty-five or thirty papers to earn a place among the more productive physiological ecologists, then I think that you could publish that review. Why not try this approach before accepting the inevitability of a "closed-door" policy?

    I will be a very poor correspondent for the next year and a half or so. I may have told you earlier that my publisher was bought out by International Thomson. The new company has decided that it wants a new edition of my book, so Peter and I are now deeply immersed in the work. It takes all of my time, and more. The present schedule calls for publication in the fall of 1983. Until then, I do not expect to get much else done.

Sincerely yours,

Edward O. Dodson

May 12, 1982

Dear Dr. Dodson:

Thanks for your April 14 answer to earlier letters. In the rush of school, my father's passing (Cincinnati, Ohio), and speaking engagements, it has taken me this long to get an answer ready—please forgive.

Point by point, it is not surprising that your biological friends object to the biology of Hoyle and Wickramasinghe, as these two men have put the finger on many things that your friends would hold as "sacred cows." It takes an outsider often to point up the underlying blind spots and weaknesses in any field. Glad you intend to read it. I hear it is difficult for some reason to get copies of this book. One friend told me they wouldn't even mail him one but insisted that the order go through a bookstore. That's a reasonable enough request, I guess. I suppose that you will probably have to place an order with your bookseller or wait until it gets onto the library shelves.

Thanks for your encouragement regarding my remarks concerning a "closed-door policy." You are right, to some measure. Just last week another paper of mine, regarding regrowth of greasewood shrubs after fire in relation to herbivore browsing, was accepted by our Southern Academy of Sciences. I just need to get a greater backlog of papers in this field and then perhaps can launch a paper on evolution pointing out some of the origins implications of the work. You are right that I should not stop trying—good advice.

Glad you are at work on your new book. If you need any help getting a little bit of scientifically based creationist ideology, I am more than willing to assist at any point. Far too few books are willing to admit that there is a vigorous minority of creation scientists at work—people who differ altogether from the atheistic and theistic evolutionists. Perhaps you will be able to get something in about this, who knows? Macroevolution models are, after all, more RELIGIOUS than they are SCIENTIFIC, so it is a pity that other scientific–religious opinions such as the Hoyle model or our own are treated as ugly step-children. It is right here that change needs to be made across the board and our colleagues really should begin treating us as scientific cohorts and, where it applies, as brothers in Christ. The various textbook writers I know try to pawn off their own RELIGIOUS opinions about origins as SCIENCE while at the same time they try to convince their naive readers that those who disagree with them are either unscientific bigots, fundamentalists, or kooks. This is academically and scientifically dishonest.

I know your time is limited but it puzzles me how a man of your deep faith in Christ, Scripture, and Catholic doctrine can rest easily with passages like Genesis 1 and 2, Exodus 20:11, and Romans 5. Sometime you can fill me in on how you rationalize ameba-to-man evolution with the doctrine of man's unique creation in Adam and Christ, the last Adam.

Best regards for a profitable year of writing,

George F. Howe

June 11, 1982

Dear Dr. Howe:

There is no need to apologize for delay in writing. As we have agreed before, we both have busy schedules, and any delays will simply be accepted as response to the unavoidable pressure of other obligations.

The book on which I am now working is simply a revision of *Evolution: Process and Product*. As a text on evolution, it is hardly a place in which I can attempt to summarize a creationist viewpoint. Actually, when I wrote my first book on evolution thirty years ago, I wanted to include a full chapter on the problem of evolution in relation to religion. The publisher vetoed it on the grounds that it was not necessary, and that, no matter what I said, it would tend to limit the potential market. Meanwhile, the public situation has changed, and I am dealing with another publisher. This time, I do intend to include a short section on the current controversies, the court challenges, etc. I shall try to be fair and conciliatory, but it will, of course, be the case for evolution which is my responsibility. I do intend to cite some books by creationists in the bibliography. At present, I plan to cite Gish, *Evolution: the Fossils Say No!*, and Morris, *Scientific Creationism*. Do you think that these are good selections? If not, can you suggest some better ones?

You asked how I reconcile my evolutionary viewpoint with Genesis 1 and 2, Exodus 20:11, and Romans 5. You will appreciate that an adequate answer would be rather time-consuming, and at present I cannot afford to take that time. However, I will try to reply adequately sometime during the summer. Meanwhile, I would like to call your attention to two of the references in *Viewpoints on Evolution and Religion*. These are the references by Hauret and Vollert, a pair of theologians whose work I have found very valuable. Unfortunately, because of their dates (1959 and 1964) you may have some difficulty in getting them. However, your librarian can probably get them on interlibrary loan from some institution in the Los Angeles area. Of the two, Hauret is the better. He states my own viewpoint far better than I could myself.

Have an ecologically productive summer.

Sincerely yours,

Edward O. Dodson

August 3, 1982

Dear Dr. Howe:

You asked how I would interpret Genesis 1 and 2, and I will try to explain in this letter. Preliminary to that, I would like to discuss Leviticus 11, in which hares are classed as ruminants and bats as birds. You are a botanist, yet I am sure that you know enough zoology to know that both of these classifications are indefensible from a scientific point of view. Did the Sacred Writer, then, err? I think not. He was simply not concerned with zoological classification. He was a spokesman for a pre-scientific culture in which the first rudiments of scientific understanding of the world in which God's people found themselves did not yet exist. To them, if an animal flew, it was a bird, and if it grazed, it was a ruminant. The Sacred Writer simply wrote within the limits of the culture of which he was a part, and he used the ordinary speech of the time to convey a message: in this case, the dietary rules of the Old Law. God could have inspired him to understand and explain scientific classification, but this would not have helped him to present his message to the Israelites. On the contrary, it would have put a stumbling block in their way. As St. Augustine put it nearly 1,600 years ago, the Scriptures tell us how to go to heaven, not how the heavens go.

It is in that frame of reference that I interpret Genesis 1 and 2. The Sacred Writer (traditionally considered to be Moses) had a message to transmit, and he did this within the framework of the culture of which he was a part. This neither presupposes nor precludes later scientific knowledge, which simply is neither necessary for nor relevant to salvation, and which would have been utterly meaningless to the Hebrews for whom Moses wrote. In Genesis 1 and 2, it was his mission to declare to the Hebrews that God created all things, including man, and that all things, and most especially the Hebrew people, were within His providence. This is God's world, and He is fully responsible for it. This must be understood, in part, in contrast to pagan systems of the time in which no one was really responsible for the world, but rather there was an inexorable fate before which even the gods were helpless. Later in Genesis, we learn that there was a fall because of disobedience, and finally there was a promise of a Redeemer to come.

These are the essentials of the early chapters of Genesis. Extremely little information is given us about the methods of creation. The symbolism of the potter is used, but that it is symbolic rather than directly descriptive is strongly indicated by the fact that it describes in purely physical terms the activity of a God who is pure spirit. Further, pottery was one of the most advanced aspects of the culture of the Hebrews, and they used the metaphor of the potter for much the same reason that modern writers use the metaphor of the computer.

A key word is *fiat*—let it be done! But the Sacred Writer does not say how it was done. Duane Gish has repeatedly said that God created by unknown processes which are no longer operative anywhere in the universe. This is a gratuitous statement which is simply not supported by the Scriptures themselves, but rather by an interpretation of the Scriptures which I believe to be as erroneous as it is gratuitous. I believe that the divine fiat set the evolutionary process in motion. This, too, is gratuitous from the viewpoint of the Scriptures, yet I believe it is at least as consistent with the Scriptures as is your interpretation. The modern concept of evolution was, of course, impossible for St. Augustine, but he came as close to it as was possible in terms of the meager science of his time. He wrote that it was inconceivable that God should have deliberately created such unpleasant things as mice and mosquitos, yet He might have permitted their formation by the operation of natural laws. He taught that, in the six days of creation, God created the *causes* of all things, but that these causes only gradually gave rise to the actual world about us. In theological terms, that is a pretty good statement of evolution, and I believe that it is every bit as

consistent with Genesis as is the current fundamentalist interpretation.

An important aspect of this discussion is the significance
of the word *day* in Genesis. We use *day* in several senses, and
so did the Hebrews. When an old man speaks of "the way things
were in my day," he is referring to all of the years from his early
youth to the height of his career. The question of the meaning
of *day* in Genesis was considered as long ago as the Babylonian
captivity by the writers of the Talmud, the Hebrew interpreters
of the Sacred Scriptures. "One day in His courts is as a thousand
years, and a thousand years as one day." In other words, to a
God who lives and works in eternity, the mortal time scale may
be meaningless. The Talmudic scholars concluded that, while
the days of creation might be days of twenty-four hours, they
might also represent periods of as much as several millions of
years, a surprisingly modern conception when one considers that
there then existed none of the geological and astronomical
knowledge which is basic to today's estimates of the duration of
time.

One of the basic principles of Catholic Biblical interpretation is that a simple, direct interpretation should be preferred
unless there is serious reason to the contrary. Serious reason may
be internal evidence—the text itself may show that a passage
is intended to be taken in a sense other than the simple, literal
one. I think that this is true of Genesis 1 and 2. The text is so
condensed, so telegraphic, that a supposed literal interpretation
requires considerable assumptions about things that are not actually stated, like Gish's assumption that unknown processes
which are no longer operative were used. Further, the use of a
then current metaphor—the potter—suggests strongly that it
is, indeed, metaphorical. There may also be external evidence.
Thus, the geological and astronomical evidences of the great
extent of time constitute serious reason to consider whether the
time scale of Genesis might have been intended in a symbolic
rather than literal sense. As nature and Genesis have the same
author, they cannot be in conflict if both are correctly interpreted.

Against this theological background, I place the great mass of modern scientific evidence that the immense variety of life developed over long reaches of time, a mass of evidence which has been sufficient to convince almost all scholars who were not convinced that it could not be true before they studied the evidence. As nature and the Bible have the same author, I can only conclude that the divine fiat set in motion an evolutionary process, that the time frame of Genesis is, as the Talmudic scholars suspected, a symbolic one rather than a sequence of twenty-four-hour days, and that, as St. Augustine taught, God created causes rather than actual objects, and that these causes only gradually produced the world as we know it. Did God have nothing to do on the eighth day? One interesting suggestion is that the eighth day is still in progress, and that it includes the grand sweep of evolution.

These, then, are the lines along which I would interpret Genesis 1 and 2. All of this is stated much better, more thoroughly, and with complete theological reasoning, by Hauret in his book, *Beginnings: Genesis and Modern Science*. I hope that you have been able to find a copy of this book which, unfortunately, is out of print. Your librarian can almost certainly find a copy, available on interlibrary loan, from some library in the Los Angeles region.

Finally, you also asked how I would interpret Exodus 20:11 and Romans 5. This has already become a very long letter, and I will not prolong it further. However, I will try to write again before the summer is over.

Sincerely yours,

Edward O. Dodson

August 9, 1982

Dear Dr. Howe:

In my last letter, I discussed the interpretation of Genesis 1 and 2. You also asked how I would interpret Exodus 20:11. This, of course, is the commandment of sabbath observance, and it begins with the statement that God created all things in six days, then rested on the seventh. As this verse depends totally on Genesis 1 and 2, the interpretation is the same, and I hardly need repeat it now. Let me just remind you that God lives and works in eternity, whereas we live and work in time. The seven days are therefore symbolic with reference to God, but the sabbath observance is a serious obligation, and an important benefit, for us.

Finally, you asked how I would interpret Romans 5. This, in my opinion, is a much more important and difficult problem. It concerns original sin, which "came into the world by one man." Catholic theologians have generally interpreted this in terms of an historical Adam from whom all mankind is descended, and from whom all have inherited the stain of original sin. This is obviously more easily interpreted in terms of a single creative act than in terms of gradual evolution. Nonetheless, the easiest interpretation is not always the correct one, and I believe that it is possible to harmonize Romans 5 with creation by means of evolution. Indeed, I believe that it is obligatory to do this in view of the weight of serious evidence in favor of evolution.

First, let me remind you that evolutionary science has long been committed to the principle of monophyly, that all of the members of a given taxonomic group share a common origin. While this is not always interpreted as a single initial pair for each species, the principle is congenial to such an interpretation. Nonetheless, current evolutionary thinking tends to emphasize the role of small populations in the origin of new species. Even if this be generally true, it would be likely that some specific cases would exemplify the minimum possible population size, a single pair, and that *H. sapiens* might be such an example. Suppose, however, that our species arose from a somewhat larger population. Could it meet the requirements of Romans 5? Quite possibly. When a very large population arises from a small initial one, crossbreeding will almost certainly result in all of the initial population being ancestral to all of the descendant population. Suppose, for example, that Adam had been the leader of an original population of ten. It would be practically impossible that he should not be ancestral to all of later humanity. Actually, there is a limited amount of internal evidence in Genesis which suggests some such solution. As you know, there has always been some debate among Christians as to whether Genesis requires the assumption of pre-Adamites. Chapters 3 and 4 speak only of the sons of Adam and Eve, yet Cain found a wife. Where did she come from? This was before the birth of Seth, " . . . another seed, for Abel, whom Cain slew" (4:25). Only in Chapter 5 does it say that "Adam . . . begot sons and daughters." I personally do not believe that these texts prove that Genesis assumes the existence of pre-Adamites. I do believe that they prove that Genesis is so elliptical that it is impossible to treat it as an adequate factual description of creation.

But is all of this necessary? In Luke 3:8, Our Lord declared that " . . . God is able from these stones to raise up children of Abraham." Might not God, then, make us children of Adam, burdened with original sin and in need of redemption, even though we owe our origin to an evolutionary process?

Original sin and our need for the Redeemer are articles of faith, obligatory for all Christians. The exact *modus operandi* of original sin is less clear. I do not pretend to know which of the above proposals is correct, nor whether some entirely different explanation may be the correct one. There are some unsolved problems, and for me this is one of them.

I must make a final comment. I am amazed at the contrast between your interpretation of the Old and New Testaments. In Genesis, you insist upon a literal interpretation in spite of serious internal and external evidence to the contrary. Yet, in the New Testament, you work hard to find symbolic or severely limited, rather than direct, literal meaning of such things as the Holy Eucharist and the commission of Peter. I think that I understand, although I disagree profoundly, your reasons for your interpretation of these New Testament passages (details in our previous correspondence). What I do not understand is how you can take so much liberty with the words of Christ Himself, then turn around and declare that similar freedom cannot be applied to the interpretation of the words of Moses. There is a profound inconsistency here. It seems to me that you are straining at a gnat and swallowing a camel.

In summary, I believe that the appearance of conflict between Christianity and science, evolutionary or other, is illusory rather than real. The proper stance of Christianity before any scientific question is one of strict neutrality because, as St. Augustine put it, the Scriptures tell us how to go to heaven, not how the heavens go. In our scientifically based society, to raise the specter of conflict between science and religion is a grave disservice to those whom we would save, and therefore to Christ, for it is not science, but religion, which is most hurt by such encounters.

Sincerely yours,

Edward O. Dodson

September 14, 1982

Dear Dr. Dodson:

Thanks for the cordial letter explaining your stance on Gen⌣₁;1 and 2. While it is important to recognize, as you pointed out, that there is considerable non-scientific or spiritual information in Genesis 1 and 2 (material we later need to realize if we wish to understand the gospel itself), Moses went a long way toward telling us that the Creator worked rapidly in a sequence involving six days that had a morning and an evening. He stressed the idea that these forms were made after their kinds and that man's body came from dust, with woman formed from man's side. It would take a greater man than Augustine to turn this around and tell us God gave very little information about *how* He created. Actually, God gave us plenty of insight on *how* He worked and it behooves you and me to listen and to accept rather than to rationalize and plead cultural frameworks. That is, it behooves us to believe this unless we want to be wrong and unless we want to displease God by our lack of faith.

There is no internal evidence in Genesis 1 and 2 to make these "days" mean anything but real days, as Exodus 20:11 would suggest. I'd sure rather let Moses interpret Scripture than Augustine. Augustine (great fellow that he was) seems to have had other problems as he bordered on spontaneous generation. Far from being "elliptical," Genesis is forthright and rather easy to understand. It is particularly easy to believe, too, if the student does not canonize the *philosophies* of evolutionary humanists *before* evaluating the Genesis text.

Now don't be too annoyed at my treatment of the Lord's Supper in this same vein. There is internal evidence to believe that Christ spoke symbolically as he passed bread and beverage to his followers as an act of obedience. But *if* I *am* wrong (as you would assert, I'm sure), do two wrongs make a right? If I am wrong in making the Lord's Supper symbolic, does that make it right for theistic evolutionists to turn Genesis 1 and 2 into symbolism when it is perfectly good Hebrew narrative prose? Does it really hurt religion when those who trust Christ as Savior also profess a living faith in the truth of God's Word? Should potential converts to Christianity be encouraged to doubt or twist the very words that Christ Himself approved? Does that really help religion or science? I wonder.

Now let me hasten to conclude that, if you persist in disagreeing with me on these points, I surely won't change my mind because I believe in letting God be true. But at the same time, I don't take it upon myself to condemn you because that isn't my task—nor do I hold any personal ill will. Nor do I suggest that your errors on these issues detract from or negate your personal salvation. I simply say that you and other theistic evolutionists are wrong on those particular points, both Biblically and scientifically.

I trust your retirement goes well. Here's a copy of my most recent chaparral paper. Keep up your studies and let me hear from you periodically. I trust your plans for a new edition go well. This book, however, should be published as a treatise in philosophy and origins rather than as a science text, since mostly it covers areas that lie outside empirical science.

Regards,

George F. Howe

November 12, 1982

Dear Dr. Howe:

I am taking a few minutes out of an extremely busy time to reply briefly to your letter of September 14. It is shocking that so much time has passed, but there just are not enough hours in the day for the writing of a major book, and unfortunately I seem to work more slowly than I did the last time around.

You and I read the clues to the interpretation of the Old and New Testaments in opposite ways. I believe that Genesis includes considerable internal evidence that it should be understood figuratively (see Hauret's book for details). Further, there is overwhelming external evidence for this from physics, astronomy, and geology, as well as the extensive evidence for evolution—and I do consider much of it to be valid scientific evidence, as do the overwhelming majority of our professional colleagues. On the other hand, there is very strong internal evidence that Our Lord meant to speak quite literally when He established the sacrament of His body and blood. He suffered the loss of many disciples because they interpreted Him literally and could not accept it. It would have been so easy to call them back with a simple explanation had He meant His words to be given the sort of figurative interpretation which you place upon them. As He did not do this, your interpretation would seem to suggest either that He failed to understand their confusion or that He had been maliciously deceptive. Both alternatives are impossible. Further, many of your fellow fundamentalists also interpret Him literally, for example, the Church of the Disciples of Christ (known simply as the Christian Church in the southeastern U.S.), in which my own grandfather and uncle were ministers.

You say that you believe "in letting God be true." Do you think that I do not? I am sure that we both do in our hearts, but I am not sure that your reasoning is consistent with that. For example, there are many physical and astronomical evidences of the great age of the universe. I have read statements by fundamentalists which begin by acknowledging the validity of these evidences and then continue to say that God created the universe a short time ago with the atomic clock, the red shift, etc., all in place as though they had had a long history. Granted that God could have done this, would it not mean that He had deliberately deceived us? And, if He has deliberately deceived us, does that not mean that He is not true but false? Of course He is not, and quite probably you reject these premises of your fellow fundamentalists. Nonetheless, I believe that there is a basic contradiction here in fundamentalist theology.

Thank you for the Xeroxes which you sent me. Young's note on "Creationism and Inerrancy" makes some of the same points which I have made before. He says that "creationists, too, stand condemned by their own charge. Not even creationists take the text literally without doing plenty of 'interpreting'. . . ." And he then gives examples. That is all for the present. I simply cannot write a long letter at this time.

Sincerely yours,

Edward O. Dodson

December 3, 1982

Dear Dr. Dodson:

Thanks for your letter of last month. I am quite sure that you are very busy, so for that reason and others I appreciate your replies to my letters. Also, it is true at this point that you are the only evolutionist I know who has courteously corresponded on these issues with me.

This is why I enjoy returning the correspondence. Although I sense in you a person who is probably just as deeply (if not more so) committed to the macroevolutionary FAITH as the others to whom I write, you alone seem to at least reflect on or even READ the things I bring to you. This is a source of some encouragement, as corresponding with other leading evolutionists is by contrast a wasteland.

I trust your book project moves along well. If you are extremely busy with that, do not feel impelled to answer this letter promptly. Let it sit in your letter stack and ferment (if you must) for a few weeks or even months. And rest assured that I understand the pressures that face a man who is active in academic, church, and family matters.

Your older book is interesting because it does contain much SCIENTIFIC EVIDENCE but in every case that evidence is in support of MICROEVOLUTION and you have not presented a shred of SCIENTIFIC EVIDENCE which *demands* MACROEVOLUTION. I was hoping that, when you produced a new volume, you could deal with what has to be a severe language problem in your tome. Moving back and forth between micro- and macroevolution may serve as a splendid mode of *indoctrination* but it can hardly be classed as an honest exercise in academics at college level. It is a means, of course, to perpetuate the misshapen idea that, if one can prove minor variations, one has established the validity of macroevolution as opposed to special creation.

Now, all of this argumentation is exactly as it should be IF macroevolution is a FAITH (akin to a religious faith) and not a SCIENCE or even a legitimate extension of SCIENCE. So I can understand, then, why you would object to introducing the special creation option or others for that matter and defend your own faith (macroevolution) to the exclusion of others. You are (perhaps unwittingly?) trying to defend a *faith* as if it were the same as or closely akin to the "science" you practise when you analyze gene systems in *Drosophila* or other forms.

Thus, the word "fundamentalist," which you used in your last letter to describe those of us who have an origins faith different from your own, probably best describes you and the other evolutionists who defend the promotion of your own origins doctrines to the exclusion of legitimate alternatives.

Your comments about evidence for vast age are a case in point. There are no "scientific data" which demand long ages but there is a plethora of conflicting data from which evolutionists have selected and popularized those points which happen to fit the preconceptions of their own origins faith.

God bless and give you a fine Christmas season.

George F. Howe

March 8, 1983

Dear Dr. Dodson:

Thanks for sending the work on Mendel, Teilhard de Chardin, and Pastushnyi. I found it most interesting and informative and it will, of course, become an important part of my file on those subjects.

Here is a published copy of my review of Hoyle and Wickramasinghe, a prepublication copy of a review of Crick's *Life Itself*, and a prepresentation copy of the abstract for my paper to be presented on May 1 at California State University, Fullerton. If my evolution-minded colleagues block my papers from their journals and even reject my letters from their columns, they must at least put up with my speeches at meetings where I am a member in good standing. Truth is not served by the fact that *Biological Abstracts* refuses to abstract ANY of our CRS papers and by the fact that rabid evolutionists block publication of creation-oriented papers. I realize you do not believe evolutionists could be guilty of such activity but, then again, the editors of *BioScience* publish your letters while rejecting mine, so I can understand your incredulity.

May you have a continuing and prosperous career.

Perhaps, too, you are not familiar with the case of young Dr. Jerry Bergman who was fired from Bowling Green State University for his scientific creationist views. He was judged the most popular teacher in his whole department and had published more than his colleagues but was denied tenure. There are numerous other illustrations of this where our "open-minded, scientific colleagues" exercise unconscionable control.

George F. Howe

May 10, 1983

Dear Dr. Howe:

I am taking advantage of a temporary lull to catch up on some correspondence. It has been many months since I wrote to you. I have never been busier. It now appears that I will be publishing *two* books next year. Last fall, Columbia University Press asked to see my Teilhard manuscript. They considered it for a long time and then, less than a month ago, they telephoned to offer me a contract for its publication. The title will be *The Phenomenon of Man Revisited: A Biological Viewpoint on Teilhard de Chardin*. While I am delighted by this turn of events, nonetheless the effort to get two major books ready for publication about the same time is pushing me pretty nearly to the limits of my capacity.

I have on hand two unanswered letters from you, and I will try to comment at least minimally on the questions which you raised in them. You speak of "moving back and forth between micro- and macroevolution . . . a splendid mode of *indoctrination* . . . ." As I think that you know, since my first book in 1952, I have tried to separate these ideas clearly, and I have expressly stated in every edition that extrapolation from micro- to macroevolution is attractive but unproven. You yourself have commended me for this. Hence, I think that the criticism is not quite fair.

Again, you say "there are no 'scientific data' which demand long ages but there is a plethora of conflicting data from which evolutionists have selected . . . those points which happen to fit [their] preconceptions . . . ." For philosophic reasons which I cannot take the time to discuss, scientific certainty is practically non-existent on any question whatever. In this sense, you are perfectly right when you say that no data "demand . . ."; however, your inference that we have simply arbitrarily selected congenial data out of an equal or greater mass of data to the contrary is simply not true. Almost all astronomers, physicists, and geologists are agreed that the great mass of applicable data in their respective fields do require great spans of time. I doubt that you could find even one of National Academy of Sciences stature who would disagree. I can appreciate your feeling that, in consideration of the measure of philosophic doubt which clouds all scientific conclusions, you must reject this conclusion for a higher reason, i.e., your interpretation of Scripture. But to simply sweep it aside as the product of biased selection of data is, I believe, a gross misrepresentation of the honest work of a very large part of the scientific community.

Elsewhere, you remark: "in their own books (your case?) they act as if a creationist origins alternative doesn't exist." At least two currently widely used evolution texts do present material on creationism. The first is Futuyma's book. It is a decidedly hostile presentation, and I question whether Futuyma knows much about it, but he definitely does not write as if the creationist alternative did not exist. The second is Stansfield's book. He quotes creationist sources at length and without critical comments, so I do not think that his book can even be called hostile. As to my own book, as I wrote to you last summer, I wanted to include a chapter on evolution and religion when I first wrote on evolution, but the publisher vetoed it. I am now dealing with a different publisher, and I wrote to you that "I do intend to include a short section on the current controversies . . . . I shall try to be fair and conciliatory, but it will, of course, be the case for evolution which is my responsibility. I do intend to cite some books by creationists in the bibliography. At present, I plan to cite Gish, *Evolution: the Fossils Say No!*, and Morris, *Scientific Creationism*. Do you think that these are good selections? If not, can you suggest some better ones?" You have not yet replied to that question.

Thank you for the abstract of your California Academy paper, and for your reviews of the books by Hoyle and Wickramasinghe and by Crick. I read them all with much interest.

This has become a longer letter than I had expected to write, but it brings me about up-to-date. Unfortunately, I am unlikely to stay up-to-date in the next year.

Sincerely yours,

Edward O. Dodson

May 26, 1983

Dear Dr. Howe:

In your letter of last December 3, you said, "Your older book is interesting because it does contain much SCIENTIFIC EVIDENCE but in every case that evidence is in support of MICROEVOLUTION and you have not presented a shred of SCIENTIFIC EVIDENCE which *demands* MACROEVOLUTION."

I have a short breathing spell now, and I would like to use part of it to comment upon your statement. First, I suppose that, by "older book," you refer to my edition of 1976, and I will reply with chapter references based upon that. I presented more scientific evidence than you seemed to realize in support of macroevolution. Chapter 1 is mainly historical, but it does include at least a trace of such evidence. Chapters 2 through 5 are primarily concerned with evidence in support of macroevolution. Chapters 7 through 12 present considerable amounts of such evidence, along with historical material. Chapter 13 is concerned primarily with microevolution, while Chapter 14 includes a major discussion of chromosomal mutations in relation to macroevolution. There is important material on macroevolution at the end of Chapter 16. Finally, Chapters 19 and 20 deal primarily with macroevolution.

So I did actually present a considerable amount of evidence in support of macroevolution. However, you qualified your statement: you said that I had not presented "a shred of SCIENTIFIC EVIDENCE which *demands* MACROEVOLUTION." Thus, the question revolves around the matter of how strong a demand you mean. If you mean a level at which the majority of qualified scientists would be convinced, then the data which I presented do demand macroevolution. If, however, you mean a level that will permit no other possible interpretation, then I agree that the evidence for macroevolution falls short of that. So does the evidence for almost all scientific phenomena. (Almost) all of science is subject to some grave philosophical reservations. I think, however, that that is not what you had in mind.

There is another aspect to this. With respect to Teilhard, I wrote that a particular statement "reveals conviction—great conviction which might well, I fear, override his scientific judgment," and you applauded that evaluation. Similarly, you have a very strong conviction that macroevolution cannot be true. Are you sure that you have not allowed that conviction to override your scientific judgment in the present case?[6]

Sincerely yours,

Edward O. Dodson

August 10, 1983

Dear Dr. Dodson:

Thanks for your kind letter—as always your good nature shows through loud and clear. Maybe there's a chance that I can convince you of your obligation to tell your readers (as you told me in your letter) that you are not really practising "science" when you discuss vast ages and propose evolutionary sequences. It seems that they should have as much right to know this as you and me and they should know that there are alternative origins models that accommodate as much or more data than general evolutionism. Leaving this out is a deliberate point of philosophical confusion. Real science is very different from the types of origins scenarios we both spin. It is a bit of an unconscious fraud on the part of evolutionists to attempt to pawn off their scenarios as scientific while either dismissing creationist scenarios as fundamentalistic or religious or even completely ignoring creationism.

Now I'm sorry I didn't send a list of publications you might cite in your book. In the middle of correspondence I have a tendency to forget some of the most important things. Why not list CRS books (see enclosed) and also the journal? If you give either or both, note the two different addresses.

Went to a Roman Catholic wedding Saturday—beautiful, worshipful, and impressive. But why did the minister say "drink ye *all* of it" for the cup and then only *he* drank? Apparently in NT times all disciples drank the cup and ate the bread together. (Pardon me, had to needle you a bit!)

My kindest regards to a fellow biologist who is cordial although evolutionistic—traits not often "linked."

George Howe

September 16, 1983

Dear Dr. Dodson:

Thanks for your letter with clipping concerning trends in the Southern Baptist Church.[7] I shall send this along to my brother, Fred Howe, who is a Southern Baptist (although he teaches theology at an independent seminary—Dallas Theological Seminary, the school where Hal Lindsey of *The Late Great Planet Earth* fame went to school).

The bald truth is that, if you believe in the literal virgin birth, sinless life, and bodily resurrection of Jesus Christ (and I am sure you do), I have much more in common with you than I have with these liberals in the Southern Baptist denomination. Several years ago, for example, there was a debate going on among students at a particular Baptist seminary as to whether or not Jesus is God. All of which goes to show that people who hold Christ pre-eminent must find their friends where they exist and this isn't always under any one denominational label. For example, I rather imagine that many of the liberal people in the Southern Baptist denomination do not hold to the verbal plenary inspiration of Scripture. This is why the conservatives are upset—they would like to regain control of what is fast slipping out of their grasp.

Our own Baptist group is an independent association of churches. No church in the GARB [General Association of Regular Baptists] automatically sends money to any denominational headquarters. Such is not true of Southern Baptists. Many of the churches send money directly to the denomination, a practice which can lead to abuses, loss of control, and a general tendency to apostatize. The Southern Baptist minister who does not believe in the bodily resurrection of Our Lord is simply not a Christian—even though he is a "Baptist." Thus, there are plenty of non-Christian Baptists, just as I would assume by the same token there are some non-Christians who profess to be Roman Catholics and yet inside doubt most, if not all, of the cardinal doctrines of Christianity. It is a strange day and time, indeed.

Then there are some who seem to hold the true gospel but abuse this in the interest of financial gain. Some of the ministers in the electronic church practise sound fiscal policies with open audits and such. Some others will have to face God for their abuse of financial matters. Glad I don't have to judge the whole mess—Catholicism and Protestantism. It's up to each of us, however, to know our mind and heart is fixed on Christ as personal redeemer and to allow His Spirit to produce in our lives what He wishes by way of a true reflection of Christ on earth.

Congratulations on your Teilhard "go-ahead." God bless. No need to hurry in answering.

George Howe

November 22, 1983

Dear Dr. Dodson:

Trust all goes well with your book writing, and other projects. I can appreciate your interest in Teilhard, as he supports your preconceived notion that, somehow, somewhere, there must be a way to combine true religion with the speculative and virtually unfounded ideas of macroevolutionism. Trust that the book will sell and that somehow some good may come of the project, although there have been very few men who have been as deeply confused in the areas of both science and religion as this poor man was.

I wonder if you have seen a very interesting article about Colin Patterson of the British Museum. He's begun to see macroevolution as some sort of bad dream when it comes to the science involved. Too bad Patterson doesn't get the kind of press that goes to Sagan and Asimov. It's not surprising, however.

My convictions concerning evolution have not overridden my scientific judgment, as you asked in an earlier letter, because there is no *scientific* evidence to support the origin of the great groups by any form of gradual evolution. The evidence points otherwise and only those who hold to macroevolution must rationalize the absence of links, negative character of mutations, rather distinct fixity of allopolyploids, inadequacy of Miller experiments to support cell origins, and so forth. John Moore wrote an interesting article on the evolutionist's cloak of ideas. I enclose it herewith.

But all this wouldn't seem so anti-scientific if my evolution colleagues were not exercising such an unethical control of media and classrooms in the free world. Colleagues who hold opposing views are given a "dirt-under-the-feet" routine and are called "religious" by people practising the religion of macroevolution. All of this is quite predictable based on human nature, and things like this have happened quite regularly in the history of science and religion—one group seeking to repress the activities and ideas of another.

Keep up your good work. Now that you are retired perhaps it would be wise to spend some time on real science as well as on the evolutionary speculations that undoubtedly call forth a tremendous share of your working hours.

It's fairly obvious that FASEB [Federation of American Societies for Experimental Biology] is practising religion when it invites a religionist of its own persuasion—C. Julian Bartlett—to write a religious article in its proceedings [42(13): 3031ff., October 1983].

God bless,

George Howe

February 21, 1984

Dear Dr. Howe:

It has been a very long time since I have written to you, and I have on hand two unanswered letters from you. I have a little time available now, and I will use it to reply at least to the first of your letters. Two major books in production at once is really a bit too much. *The Phenomenon of Man Revisited* will soon be published, and that will help.

Evidently, I did not make myself clear in my letter of last May 26, for you say: "Maybe there's a chance that I can convince you of your obligation to tell your readers (as you told me in your letter) that you are not really practising 'science' when you discuss vast ages and propose evolutionary sequences." I really didn't say that. What I said was that the data of macroevolution fall short of the level of proof which will admit of no other possible interpretation. I said also that the level of proof attained is sufficient to convince the majority of qualified scientists, and I think that that is not quite consistent with the interpretation which you put on my remark. I may add that I have always included such qualifications in my book (i.e., that the data are subject to varying interpretations, or that the data are inadequate at a specific point, etc.), and, if anything, those words of caution will be stronger this time than in earlier editions.

Further, this time I have even included some information on creationism—not much, to be sure, and from the viewpoint of a student of evolution—but I think that the material is fair, and I have also included references which were written by creationists.

Returning to my letter of last May 26 and your comments upon it, I also said that "(Almost) all of science is subject to some grave philosophical reservations." You wrote a note on this, but it did not Xerox well. Let me expand upon that a little. When he steps into his laboratory, every scientist tacitly makes a series of five fundamental suppositions, as follows: (1) that nature is orderly; (2) that the order of nature is discoverable; (3) that sensory evidence is at least potentially reliable; (4) that nature is adequately describable in terms of space, time, energy, and mass, the only terms which science has at its disposal; and (5) that the human mind, working according to the laws of logic, is a trustworthy instrument. Not one of these has ever been proven, and perhaps they are unprovable, yet every scientist makes an act of faith in all of them, usually unconsciously, every time he steps into his laboratory.

In the same letter, you mentioned having gone to a Catholic wedding, and I was pleased that you found it "beautiful, worshipful, and impressive." But you wondered why only the priest took the cup, while the people received only the consecrated bread. First, let me say that I am really surprised, because the current tendency is to share the cup more widely, and at weddings the bridal couple is almost always given communion under both kinds. But American Catholics tend to be more conservative than I have found them either in Canada or in Europe. You must have visited a very conservative parish indeed.

Going beyond that, there is a long history. As you say, in the early Church, communion was ordinarily under both kinds. Later, there was even a time when reception under both kinds was required. This was in response to a heresy according to which it was wrong to receive the consecrated wine because of its alcoholic content. The practice of distributing only the consecrated bread arose during times of pestilence in the late Middle Ages. Of course, the germ theory of disease was unknown, but still it became evident that the common cup had something to do with the epidemics. The theological principle is that Christ is received whole and entire under either kind. Our Lord's instructions, if you read the original Greek text, are not quite as clear as you suggest, for some of the original texts say "body and blood," while others say "body *or* blood."

You add that "what I really hope is that Catholics trust Christ and not a wafer." This is a theme to which you have returned several times, and I think that you should put your fears to rest. That Christ is truly present in the sacrament of His body and blood is a major theme of Catholic education; that the child is able to distinguish the consecrated host from ordinary bread is the most important requirement for eligibility for first communion. The Mass itself includes numerous reminders of this fact and, at the moment of reception, the priest (or other minister of the sacrament) tells each communicant, "The body of Christ," to which the communicant replies, "Amen." With all of this, it would require a certain perverse genius to place the pastry ahead of Christ. Catholics who do so may be even rarer than Baptists who do not distinguish the waters of baptism from the Saturday night bath.

So I suggest that you stop worrying about whether Catholics replace faith in Christ with faith in a wafer. It is only because "who eats my flesh and drinks my blood abides in me and I in him" (John 6:56) that we place importance upon Holy Communion. Rather, do some worrying about those of your fellow Baptists who find themselves censured by Our Lord in John 6:53, " . . . unless you eat the flesh of the Son of Man and drink his blood, you have not life in you"; or by 1 Cor. 11:27 and 29, "So that whoever eats the bread or drinks the cup of the Lord unworthily shall be guilty of the body and blood of the Lord . . . for he that eats and drinks without distinguishing the body from other food, eats and drinks judgment to himself."

This is a longer letter than I really intended to write. I hope that I can answer the other letter without so long a delay.

Sincerely yours,

Edward O. Dodson

P.S. Just a very brief note in reply to your letter of Sept. 16, and I will be caught up. Catholics recite the Apostles' or Nicene Creed every Sunday, and we expect our members to believe the tenets of the creeds, including the virgin birth, the crucifixion and resurrection, and the Godhood of Jesus Christ. We strive for a sinless life, but most of us fail, and we rely on the forgiveness of God. One good result of the Council back in the sixties is that most of the nominal Catholics left the Church, so that there are now fewer but more devout Catholics.

June 7, 1984

Dear Dr. Howe:

I have a brief lull between books now, and I will use it to catch up on correspondence. Perhaps you saw the ad for Columbia University Press in *Science* for May 18, and if so you know that my Teilhardian book is now available. Perhaps you will review it for *CRSQ* or elsewhere. We are now deeply into production work for *Evolution*, but at the moment I have completed my part until they send me the next batch of edited manuscript.

When I last wrote to you (February 21, 1984!), I said that my letter brought me up-to-date. I was in error, for I soon discovered your letter of November 22, 1983, on my desk (a center of confusion where things can easily get lost). You said that "I can appreciate your interest in Teilhard, as he supports your preconceived notion that, somehow, somewhere, there must be a way to combine true religion with the speculative and virtually unfounded ideas of macroevolutionism . . . very few men . . . have been as deeply confused in . . . both science and religion as this poor man was." When you read my book, *The Phenomenon of Man Revisited: A Biological Viewpoint on Teilhard de Chardin*, you will be at risk of revising your opinion of Teilhard for the better!

As to the "speculative and virtually unfounded ideas of macroevolutionism," we have discussed this before. The fact is that there is very extensive evidence in support of macroevolution, evidence which is respected by almost all biologists who are not fundamentalists. I have included an elementary review of a sample of that evidence in my new book, and we have done the same thing more extensively in the new edition of *Evolution*, which will probably appear early in 1985. We are agreed that the evidence for macroevolution is less complete than that for microevolution, and that much of it is indirect (in common with much scientific evidence, for example all of that for atomic theory). You regard it as not only indirect but wholly inadequate; in common with most of our professional colleagues, I regard it as a fact of nature concerning which, however, many of the most interesting questions remain to be answered by future research.

You suggest that Colin Patterson and other evolutionary biologists are beginning to see macroevolution as a "bad dream." Sunderland's article gives that impression, but I do not trust short quotations out of context. I would like to see Patterson's evaluation of Sunderland's report on Patterson's thinking. A couple of years ago, I had the pleasure of reviewing a popular book on evolution by Patterson. The contents of that book are not recognizable in Sunderland's article. Perhaps Patterson's thinking metamorphosed overnight; that would be necessary if Sunderland's article is to be valid.

Sunderland is also impressed by Hoyle and Wickramasinghe. I frankly do not know why. They simply move the locale of the origin of life from the earth to outer space but, once those primal germs of life reached the earth, it would require prodigious evolution to produce the world of life as we know it. Wickramasinghe was the star witness for the creationists at the Arkansas trial, yet when he was asked if it were possible that the world was less than a million years old, he replied with an emphatic *no*. I would think that creationists would find cold comfort in the testimony of these men.

Contrary to your declaration, there is indeed much scientific evidence of macroevolution, and almost all biologists who are not fundamentalists agree on this. You cited specifically "absence of links, negative character of mutations, rather distinct fixity of allopolyploids, inadequacy of Miller experiments to support cell origins . . . ." All of these points are covered in my book, *Evolution*, but I will comment briefly on each. First, while it is true that the number of known fossil links between major groups is disappointingly small, there are good cases. *Archeopteryx* is a bird that shares more characteristics with reptiles (whether fossil or living) than it does with living birds.

There are many fossils which have been classified as amphibians or as reptiles at different times, even by the same investigator. It is still controversial among specialists on reptiles and mammals where the line should be drawn between these classes in the fossil record. All of these cases of difficult decision, indecision, and fluctuating decision bespeak intermediacy. If these are not good links between the classes, then I really don't know how such links should be defined.

The "negative character of mutations" is grossly exaggerated by creationists. While it is true that most mutations are harmful and that their prospective fate is elimination by natural selection, there is a small residue of valuable mutations. If this were not so, plant and animal breeding would be a waste of time. The breeders exploit those positive mutations which form the basis for improvement of stocks. Also, whether a mutation is harmful or beneficial often depends upon environmental factors, as in the famous case of the pepper moths. I do not know what you mean by "rather distinct fixity of allopolyploids." They represent incontrovertible origin of new species and genera, and Stebbins cites probable cases of new families arising by this means. Thus, allopolyploidy is demonstrated macroevolution.

As to the "inadequacy of Miller experiments to support cell origins," they were never meant to do this. On the contrary, they were meant to demonstrate the possibility of the origin of a variety of biochemical compounds under the abiotic conditions of the primitive earth. They were quite successful in doing this. Presumably, these compounds might then be used in the origin of cells, but that is another problem. As all of these things are agreed by the great majority of our professional colleagues, I think that it is fair to say that you may have allowed your religious convictions to override your professional judgment in much the same fashion that Teilhard sometimes allowed his convictions to override his scientific judgment.

Next, you complain: "Colleagues who hold opposing views are given the 'dirt-under-the-feet' routine . . . one group seeking to repress the activities and ideas of another." Unfortunately, there is too much truth to that, but it is not so specifically directed against scientists who are creationists as you think. You may remember that, about a year and a half ago, *Science* published a series of articles on a controversy among ecologists, and it mentioned that proponents of the opposed views were not on speaking terms. For another example, a book review by C.A.B. Smith includes the following:

> As a student I . . . was vaguely aware that the pioneering work had been done by R. A. Fisher, J.B.S. Haldane, and Lancelot Hogben . . . I had a rosy vision of Fisher, Haldane, and Hogben frequently discussing, with great excitement, their latest discoveries and plans for the future.
>
> In fact . . . fate decreed that I should become a mathematical geneticist and get to know Fisher, Haldane, and Hogben personally . . . . What immediately became clear was that relations between them were alas far from ideally cordial and that each . . . could sometimes be inexplicably prickly, hindering both intellectual contact and scientific advance.

Of course, such personal ill will among differing colleagues ought not to exist. It should be possible to disagree with mutual respect and goodwill, as I believe that you and I do. But it is human, and you as creationists are by no means its sole victims. And there is an antidote which I have recommended before: publication of objective scientific works. My colleague Vadim D. Vladykov, for example, is a creationist who is a world authority on ichthyology. Few people have published as much solid work on fishes as he has. He commands the respect of all ichthyologists. Your colleague, the physiologist Smith, is working for similar eminence in his field. And you should be doing the same thing in physiological ecology. A scientist with fifty good, solid, objective papers to his credit can usually get a respectful hearing even if his colleagues disagree strongly.

Well, that is enough for the present.

Sincerely yours,

Edward O. Dodson

July 7, 1984

Hi, Dr. Dodson:

I am sure my recent material on Teilhard reached you, as I got a letter from you that must have crossed in the mail. I surely appreciate your correspondence and find that you are perhaps the one outstanding exception I have to "Howe's Law," which goes as follows:

> Evolutionists are long on *ad hominem* arguments against creationists and prefer to deal in scurrilous attacks rather than the scientific data they profess to handle. Furthermore, evolutionists will cut you off in correspondence as soon as the going gets a bit too tough for them.

You, sir, are the exception.

Now, I appreciate the Feb. 21 letter which I really haven't answered yet. Let me do so now.

Thanks for filling me in on the open and honest way you have admitted the uncertainties in evolution*ism* and for the fact that you have mentioned creationists in your book. I shall write to the publisher to see if I can secure a complimentary copy of the book for possible adoption next time I teach origins.

All of what you say about "faith" in true science is true and I agree. The point I have been trying to make, however, is that there is *another level* of faith (additional faith) that colors all origins study; hence we are not dealing with true science when we discuss origins but with another field that has much more faith involved than the five steps you list. I will not be silent until more and more of my secular colleagues (and religious ones as well) will come right out and admit that origins is not "science" in the usual sense of that latter word.

I enjoyed your discussion of how the use of the cup by the laity has varied over the years—all of this is quite understandable.

I hope you are right that most Catholics trust in THE CHRIST and not in some symbols that He established to commemorate the reality of His shed blood, redemption, and saving grace.

The verse used here (John 6:56) is undoubtedly figurative and does not refer to what you call Holy Communion. Context demonstrates the figurative character of Christ's words. Once again I find it interesting that you have a habit of missing the figurative character of references like this while trying to turn Genesis 1 and 2 into a figurative account, when it is obviously clear-cut narrative. But we all have our problems, I suppose, and I can overlook this problem in one who otherwise takes a gracious approach to those who obviously disagree with him.

1 Cor. 11:27 and 29 refer to those who come with unconfessed sin and otherwise treat the communion service disrespectfully. You would not believe how many sermons are preached on this in Baptist churches—I daresay far more than Catholic kids get in their catechismal classes.

I rejoice that Catholics recite a creed that contains basic truth. Once again I hope that such repetitive observance does not cloud or obfuscate the true process of being "born again" (Christ's own words to Nicodemus). I am sure in many cases they do not and we have Catholics who understand what it means to have a living relationship with Christ as Savior.

Now we must turn to your good letter of June 7.

Thanks for the word on the Teilhard manuscript. Would it be possible for your publisher or you to send me what is called a "review copy"? Quite often those who wish me to review books for *CRSQ* do just that. I want to review the book for CRS and will do so ultimately, you can be sure.

Ah, surely you have "evidence for macroevolution" in that you can take data of genetics and paleontology and fit them into the macro schema. What I am asking you to produce is evidence that CANNOT be explained equally as well or even better by those lousy "fundamentalists" who seem to be the only ones with guts enough to challenge a monolithic establishment. When I see the evidence that supports macroevolution and macro only (to the exclusion of a rational creationist alternative explanation) I will be duly impressed.

I wish I had Sunderland's address. As soon as I can get hold of it, I will send along a copy of the full address. Meanwhile, you will find hardly any context in which Patterson's words could be considered supportive of the kind of macroevolution that is so falsely promoted as "science" in schoolrooms around the world.

With the utmost respect let me state that in certain paragraphs in your letter I see you doing here what anyone will do under pressure—minimize the force of arguments which run slap counter to one's ruling origins view. We cherish these origins views almost as deeply as our Sunday creeds and therefore I can understand why you are unimpressed when you see that the very foundations of macroevolution ideology are rotten.

Thank you for this treatise on the fact that it is HUMAN, not just evolutionist, to practise ill will to one's fellow man. I realize this but forget it now and then. Here it is that you and I (but probably not Teilhard) would agree on the Biblical doctrine of the Fall of Man and that we have, even as believers, what Paul calls an "old man" or old nature. We know also that it is really only through the redeeming power of Jesus Christ that evolutionist and creationist can calmly (as we do in letters) discuss differences and each set to work without rancor. We can only trust and pray that more and more of these evolutionists and scientists in general will look to God's risen Lamb for a life-changing experience.

God's blessing to you and please do tell me when your book rolls off the press.

George Howe

July 23, 1984

Dear Dr. Howe:

Once again, I have a little respite from proofs, etc., and I find that I owe you *two* letters. The first, dated June 13, was very brief, serving mainly to enclose a Xeroxed report of Winslow's idea that Conan Doyle was the culprit in the Piltdown hoax. You are right, I was not aware of that theory when I wrote my Piltdown paper. About a year ago, however, Winslow himself wrote to tell me that he planned to publish his paper implicating Conan Doyle. There seem to be a large number of people who might have done it, and very little specific evidence to implicate any of them.

Then you spoke of your pleasure in reading Pascal, and you added a curious gibe: "Then I got to thinking that, if I was finding so much of personal spiritual value in Pascal, he is probably judged heretical by Catholics???" I remembered Pascal as being highly regarded in the Church but, to make sure of my ground, I read the article on Pascal in the *Catholic Encyclopedia*. I found him discussed in wholly laudatory terms, even mentioning the possibility of sainthood. Perhaps your pleasure in reading Pascal shows that you have more in common with Catholics and Catholic faith than you realize—or like to admit. Some time ago, you said that you were not protesting anything (i.e., you were not Protestant in the root sense). More recently, you pointed out, in relation to a news item on the Southern Baptist Convention, that there are Baptists whom you would not even consider to be Christians (because they deny the divinity of Christ). Accordingly, you said that you had more in common with Bible-oriented Catholics than with some Baptists. Yet, you keep returning to things like the present gibe. In spite of the things mentioned above, you seem to be preoccupied with motes in Catholic eyes, yet you seem quite unconcerned about beams in Baptist eyes.

Your second letter was undated, but it was postmarked July 7. You asked about my books. First, my Teilhardian book has been published by Columbia University Press. The title is *The Phenomenon of Man Revisited: A Biological Viewpoint on Teilhard de Chardin.* I'm sorry that I do not have a copy that I can send you. They gave me twelve copies but, by the time I had given a copy to each of my children and to several people to whom I am indebted for valuable assistance with the book, they were all gone. If the editor of *CRSQ*, or of any other journal for which you might review it, will write to CUP and request a review copy, I am sure that they will get it.

The new edition of *Evolution: Process and Product* is now in galley proofs, and it is scheduled for publication early in 1985. Reinhold was bought, along with the rest of the publishing interests of the Litton Corporation, by International Thomson. Hence, the new edition is in the hands of one of their subsidiaries, PWS Publishers of Boston. Again, you can get a review copy in the same way.

Much of your letter was given over to discussion of my letters of February 21 and June 7. I am pleased to note that we have considerable areas of agreement. At the risk of being a bit tedious, I will return to a few points on which we are not in agreement. You say that John 6:56 is shown by context to be figurative, but you cite nothing in the context as evidence of this. I do not believe that there is such evidence in the context. I have already discussed the opposed view in several letters (May 15 and October 16, 1981, and November 12, 1982), so I will summarize tersely now. When Our Lord foretold the sacrament of His body and blood, many of the disciples said that "This is a hard saying," and they left Him. He could easily have recalled them by explaining that He meant it figuratively, but He let them go rather than soften His "hard saying." If your interpretation is correct, then His failure to recall them with a softer word must mean either that He failed to understand their confusion, or that He had maliciously deceived them. As I must consider both of these alternatives to be impossible contradictions of His divine nature, I can only conclude that Our Lord was quite conscious of speaking literally rather than figuratively.

With respect to 1 Corinthians 11:27 and 29, you are quite right that these "refer to those who come with unconfessed sin and otherwise treat the communion service disrespectfully." This is a good Catholic doctrine, as taught both in catechism classes and in countless sermons. Are you so sure, though, that it may not be disrespectful to treat the communion service as very much less important than Christ Himself declared it to be, and the elements of communion as mere symbols if, in fact, they are what Christ declared them to be, His true body and blood?[8]

In your letter of last November, you had cited several categories of evidence that you considered an embarrassment to evolutionary biologists. In my letter of June 7, I stated rather tersely why I think that you are in error on this, some of these categories (allopolyploidy, for example) being decidedly in favor of macroevolution. In reply, you say that "I see you doing here what anyone will do under pressure—minimize the force of arguments which run slap counter to one's ruling origins view." Pardon me, but I think that the shoe is on the other foot. All of these categories of evidence to which you refer do, in fact, support macroevolution. Creationists are clutching at straws when they seize upon the incompleteness of some of these lines of evidence—most of them. The data are good but, like most areas of active research, incomplete. In one case, however, allopolyploidy, the data are sufficiently complete that Stebbins dropped his research in this field in favor of developmental aspects of evolution because he felt that the role of allopolyploidy in macroevolution was so fully understood that only minor details and additional examples need be added. Much of creationist literature consists of a nit-picking search for flaws in evolutionary studies.

Continuing the quotation in the preceding paragraph, you said: "We cherish these origins views almost as deeply as our Sunday creeds . . . . " This, I think, is your real point, and I respect it as a forthright declaration of faith. As a tenet of faith,

I think that it is erroneous, but it deserves respect because it is sincerely held. The effort to clothe this declaration of faith in the trappings of science has not, in my opinion, done your cause good, as witness the array of current books in which many scientists are defending evolutionary science against what they decry as creation science. Finally, we are agreed that, after the Fall, scientists like all others stand in need of the redemptive sacrifice of Christ, the Lamb of God who takes away the sins of the world.

Sincerely yours,

Edward O. Dodson

September 4, 1984

Dear Dr. Howe:

Thank you for sending me the text of Colin Patterson's speech of November 5, 1981, given at the American Museum of Natural History. The quotations that you sent me previously are, indeed, representative of the whole speech; and they are, as I remarked earlier, inconsistent with his recent book, *Evolution*. He himself explains this when he says: "One morning I woke up and something had happened in the night, and it struck me that I had been working on this stuff for twenty years and there was not one thing I knew about it."

Fair enough. Anyone has a right to change his mind. However, I have some problems with that speech. Not the least of these is rather poor grammar and diction. This may be accounted for by the fact that this is a transcript of an oral presentation that has not benefitted from editing, unlike his published works. Patterson, however, is a highly educated English gentleman with a doctorate from the University of London. Such people typically speak as beautifully as they write.

Another problem is his statement that he got no answers when he asked his question, "Can you tell me anything that you know about evolution . . . any one thing that is true?" He asked this question before the geology staff of the Field Museum of Natural History and the Evolutionary Morphology Seminar of the University of Chicago, both of which include a number of people who think that they know quite a lot that is true about evolution. Some of them have committed themselves publicly many times. Why not this time? One has to wonder if the question might not have been so posed that it appeared to be a rhetorical question, so that no answer was expected other than that of the speaker himself.

Another thing that troubles me is that this paleontologist says nothing about paleontology but quite a lot about protein homologies and their supposed inconsistency with evolution. I found his presentation of the data not sufficiently clear that I could satisfy myself as to whether his argument was or was not correct. Perhaps I will be persuaded when I have restudied it. For the present, I have to contrast it with the clear studies of Barker and Dayhoff, Doolittle, and Fitch and Margoliash, all of which give clear evidence of evolution. When a specialist in one field draws his data and examples primarily from another field in which he can claim no special expertise, I always wonder whether he is on secure ground.

Third, I was at first perplexed by Patterson's repeated references to "Conbear's law." The law, or principle, I know well and use in my book on evolution: that in embryonic development, general characteristics appear first, then the less general, and finally the particular characteristics. But I associate this principle with the name of Karl Ernst von Baer. Then I realized that "Conbear" was almost certainly an error of transcription of "von Baer."

Finally, you wrote a note on the Patterson text: "We find it surprising as creationists that you and many other evolutionists do not take as *open* and objective an attitude as this great paleontologist." I think that the answer is quite simple: to be convinced of anything is a restriction on one's openness to any opposed principle. I suspect that you are no more open than I am to persuasion by the Jehovah's Witnesses and Mormons who call at our doors from time to time. We evolutionary biologists have surveyed the evidence for evolution and we have found it convincing. We have not found similar scientific merit in the evidence presented by scientific creationists. Similarly, I am convinced that the earth is round, although there is a Flat Earth Society, the members of which deplore the lack of openness to what they regard as evidence to the contrary; I am convinced that the atomic theory of matter is correct, although no one has ever seen an atom; and I am convinced that the variety of life arose by an evolutionary process because a considerable number of independent lines of evidence point toward that conclusion with high levels of probability and because, in two cases, the many examples of allopolyploid plants and the species of the *Drosophila pseudoobscura*[9] group, origin of new species by evolutionary processes is proven beyond a reasonable doubt.

Nor do I regard this as inconsistent with divine creation. As you know, I believe that God is the Creator of all things, but I also believe that evolution is His method of creation of the wonderful variety of life. I think that the late Theodosius Dobzhansky, the Dean of modern evolutionary biologists and a very devout man, would have agreed with me. We might be tempted to ask why you creationists are not more open and objective toward this sublime possibility.

Sincerely yours,

Edward O. Dodson

November 1, 1984

Dear Dr. Howe:

After you sent me the transcript of Colin Patterson's seminar at the American Museum of Natural History, in which he seemed to have moved close to a creationist position, I wrote to Patterson. I asked him two questions: (1) is the transcript [I sent him the first few pages of it] reasonably accurate; and (2) does it represent your current thinking on the subject?

I have now received his reply, and you may find it disappointing. On the first question, he says that the transcript is "garbled and nonsensical in places . . . but I think it is roughly accurate." He replies to the second question with a categorical "No." He had thought that he was talking only to a group of professional systematists and he was deliberately presenting a viewpoint calculated to provoke discussion. He refers to "infiltration by creationists" and to "surreptitious use of tape recorders." His conclusion is that "treating evolutionary theory as axiomatic has not been beneficial in systematics, but I am in no way a creationist, and have no respect for the views or arguments of the creationist lobby."

The first part of that sentence is not very different from Simpson's statement forty years ago that the taxonomic system was devised without reference to evolutionary theory and that it is notably ill-adapted for the expression of evolutionary relationships. Nobody accused Simpson of creationist leanings. The second part is an unconditional repudiation by Patterson of the interpretation which you and Sunderland placed upon Patterson's seminar. I agree that the transcript, considered in isolation, would seem to justify your interpretation. I am enclosing a Xerox copy of his letter, and you can see for yourself what Patterson has to say.

One further comment: Patterson refers to "surreptitious use of tape recorders." Evidently, Sunderland did not ask for permission to record the seminar. He should know that it is illegal to record—and especially to distribute transcripts of the recording—without the permission of the speaker.

Under separate cover, I have sent you a short monograph which the American Teilhard Association asked me to write on Teilhard and Mendel. I think that you will find some material of interest in it, particularly in the sections on Mendel.

Sincerely yours,

Edward O. Dodson

February 17, 1985

Dear Dr. Dodson:

Thanks for the complimentary copy of your book on Teilhard and Mendel which I am in the process of reading. Also I appreciated reading the copy of Patterson's reply to you. As I indicated, I have gotten into contact with Sunderland to answer some questions in my own mind. The whole foundation of the macroevolution concept is rotten, no matter what Dr. Colin Patterson says or believes. The point is, however, that Dr. Patterson *did* say that he saw evolution as little more than a bad dream. Then, in your letter of July 7, you said that you did not trust short quotations out of context. I replied that it would be very hard to understand Dr. Patterson's words as being anything but critical of evolution in ANY context.

I located Mr. Sunderland and sent you a copy of a transcript of the talk that Patterson gave. Then, after reading this transcript, you (in a very lengthy letter of Sept. 4) indicated that you too were puzzled over how an avowed evolutionist could speak like this. You preferred (instead of looking at the problems he raised) to rest on more orthodox authorities like Doolittle, who chant the usual transformist party lines and minimize any problems that keep coming up.

Then you wrote a pointed little letter of Nov. 1 in which you sent the reply of Dr. Patterson to a letter you had sent to him. You singled out Patterson's comment about "surreptitious use of tape recorders," and you said, "Evidently, Sunderland did not ask for permission to record the seminar . . ." and you made some remarks about the legality or illegality of taping without permission and distributing transcripts of tapes.

Let's be Biblical and let the "last be first." You were sent a transcript of the tape because *you* had raised questions about the context of remarks in a published article. I secured a copy of the transcript and sent it to you for scholarly purposes. Now that you have made your use of the document, please send my copy back at your soonest convenience. Under United States law (our counsel tells us), it is perfectly legal to tape a meeting that is open to the public, as these seminars obviously are. Mr. Sunderland did not tape the session himself but writes: "For your information, I did not attend or tape Patterson's talk. It was taped by at least two people; one was a regular member of the Systematics Group and the other was a guest. I have never sold copies of the tape or the taped transcript." Sunderland then goes on to tell the name and address of the man who received the tape from the member of the seminar and who, for a fee, will supply a copy of the tape to anyone who writes. Thus, in answer to your November letter, this pattern Sunderland followed was far from "distributing transcripts of the recording," and since you have evidently satisfied whatever real scientific curiosity you originally had in finding out what Dr. Patterson said, I will repeat that it would be appreciated if you were to send back my copy of the transcript.

Mr. Sunderland is highly ethical and writes, "I did, out of courtesy, send Dr. Patterson a copy of my article for him to correct any misquotations, but he made no corrections." He also writes, "Dr. Patterson told me in London on June 22, 1982, that my article about his talk at the American Museum had generated such a flood of letters that he wanted to write an article explaining why he said what he did. Did I think *Acts & Facts* would print it? I checked with Henry Morris who naturally agreed. After writing to Dr. Patterson and informing him that he should write the article, I never heard from him again. Several years later, a friend of mine had lunch with Dr. Patterson and asked him what had happened. Dr. Patterson told him that his superiors would not permit him to publish the article and told him to cool it."

Now, along this line, I suspect that creationists and evolutionary-critics-of-evolutionism in England are just as much (if not more so) subject to harassment by supervisors and their professional colleagues as we are here in America. I suspect that both Patterson and Popper have been harassed by their peers who are dogmatic evolutionists—a very cruel but not unusual practice. I do not suspect you did this sort of thing in the letter you sent Patterson, but then you did not send me a copy of *your* letters to Patterson so I do not know exactly how you couched this matter to him. I do know that MANY *other* evolutionists have browbeaten their critical or creationist colleagues in a manner unworthy of scientists and/or scholars.

But aside from this important issue, both you and Patterson must remember one thing—none of us (Sunderland or me) has quoted Patterson "as if he were a creationist . . . ." We know full well that Patterson IS an EVOLUTIONIST and THEREFORE we find his criticisms and conclusions most fascinating as they come from the mouth of an otherwise hostile witness, as would be said in court. In one fell swoop he refutes statements of yours in which you gloss over the wholesale problems faced by evolutionists and try to convince us and the public that creationists are mere nit-pickers.

Well, the truth of these gross problems "will out," my friend, despite your attempts to minimize them and despite the fact that you have probably avoided them in your new edition as surely as you did in the earlier ones. But Patterson is a "different breed of cat" and has at the same time let the "cat" out of the bag, as you will find by looking at his *Harper's* magazine article (February). Evidently Patterson speaks much more openly about the grossities of the macroevolution model than he would want you to think in his letter. Why don't you write to him and ask him what he thinks or what he means by his rather forthright criticisms of evolutionism in the *Harper's* article by Bethell? This individual who would have you think that he was the victim of those who make " . . . surreptitious use of tape recorders . . . " (in open meetings, by members of that very seminar) evidently speaks quite plainly against evolution to journalists like Bethell as well. Surely, if what he says about paleontology fits better with our origins model than yours, you cannot deny us the right of quoting him. Evidently the transcript of Patterson's speech, together with Bethell's article, justifies *our* interpretation of what he is really saying rather than yours.

Yours for an approach to origins that is more open and more worthy of real scholars,

George F. Howe

P.S. Perhaps instead of writing any more letters to Dr. Patterson to find out what he really means, you should begin trying to solve some of the weighty problems he points out for evolutionists. Also, rather than trying to see if they can trump up some ethical problems about creationists' use of quotations, evolutionists in general would do well to practise academic openness and set to work themselves SHARING and attempting to solve the problems that are legion. At this point, the public and the creationists might be a little more willing to say that evolutionists were acting like scientists rather than like the religionists they really are.

April 10, 1985

Dear Dr. Howe:

We all have our better and worse days, and I think that you had a bad one when you wrote to me on February 17. The tone of your letter was hostile, in contrast to that of our correspondence in general. There seem to be two bases for your anger. First, I quoted Dr. Patterson's remarks on "infiltration [of the meeting] by creationists" and "surreptitious use of tape recorders." You seem to be applying a double standard here: it is fair to quote Patterson to indicate confusion and dissension among evolutionary biologists, but it is not fair to quote him against creationists. It was you who introduced the subject of the Patterson seminar, and I am sure that, after a little reflection, you will agree that it is also fair to quote his remarks about his seminar.

You added that you had not seen my letter to Patterson. You kindly mentioned that you did not suspect me of browbeating him, but that this cruel practice was not unusual. I did not send you copies of my *two* letters to Patterson because they were very brief, my quotation was nearly complete, and it did not seem worthwhile to Xerox them. I enclose the Xeroxes now, and you can verify that I did not pressure him in any way.

Second, you seemed angry because I had questioned the legality of recording the seminar without the speaker's knowledge or permission. I think that this is a reasonable question, and I raised it in goodwill. I'm sorry that you did not accept it that way. Occasionally, someone asks my permission to record my lectures. I always agree—I cannot quite imagine refusing—but I would be offended if it were done without my knowledge and permission. On one occasion, I was told that the tape was intended for the use of creationists. I still agreed. Under Canadian law, lectures are specifically protected by copyright, even if the author does not register the copyright. The advantage to registration is that the certificate is legal evidence in event of contest. American copyright law was thoroughly revised a few years ago, and I know little about it. Under Canadian law, it would probably be a violation of copyright to tape a lecture without the permission of the speaker. I have not consulted a lawyer about this, but I have read the law.

In your postscript, you speak of evolutionists trumping up "ethical problems about creationists' use of quotations." I certainly have not meant to suggest that use of quotations is not legitimate. Indeed, I think that it is necessary if you are trying to counter someone's views, but that is quite different from taping lectures without the knowledge or permission of the speaker. One of the few things that I do know about current U.S. copyright law is that it provides for "fair use" without permission. What constitutes fair use is not defined in the law, but the editors at Columbia University Press told me that norms of the industry sanction quotations of not more than 500 words in any one passage, not more than 2,500 words in all quotations from a single work, and never a complete work even if it is very short (a sonnet, for example). That leaves a lot of room for direct quotation and, as long as the quotation does not misrepresent the intention of the author, it is, subject to the above limitations, fair and proper.

After all of that quasi-legal discussion, let me add that Sunderland is undoubtedly right that it makes an important difference that the tapes were not sold. And I am glad to know that he sent his article to Patterson—a nice courtesy. I had assumed that it was Sunderland who had recorded the seminar because his was the only name that you had mentioned. I was wrong, and I am sorry.

Thank you for sending me the article from *Harper's* magazine. I read it with much interest. I see it primarily as documentation of a squabble among taxonomists, the cladists vs. all others. In his letter to me, Patterson said, "I still hold the view that treating evolutionary theory as axiomatic has not been beneficial in systematics." I agree with him; in fact, I would go much further—I don't think that it is beneficial to treat evolution as axiomatic in any branch of biology, and least of all in evolutionary biology. It is a working hypothesis and a proposition to be tested, not an axiom, which is a self-evident truth. I can well understand that you would find the *Harper's* article very gratifying. I cannot agree with you, however, that "in one fell swoop he refutes statements of yours in which you gloss over the wholesale problems faced by evolutionists and try to convince us and the public that creationists are mere nit-pickers!" One paper cannot sweep away over a century of research and thousands of papers "in one fell swoop." Despite the controversy over cladism, there is still a vast array of evidence for evolution, drawn from such diverse fields as biogeography, comparative anatomy, comparative embryology, comparative physiology, comparative biochemistry, paleontology, genetics, and cytology. Indeed, much of the evidence from taxonomy is untroubled by the controversy over cladism. Incidentally, I have never said that "creationists are mere nit-pickers." I do think, however, that creationists tend to underestimate the evidence for evolution and to overestimate the "gross problems" of evolutionary biology. There are, of course, many unsolved problems. It would be sad if there were not, for there would be no challenges for young researchers. Evolution has been an extremely productive working hypothesis. The accumulated data from many areas of biological research have convinced the great majority of biologists that evolution is a fact of nature. Against that background, you have told me on several occasions that there really isn't any such evidence. You would be more convincing if you would acknowledge the evidence, but argue that it was mostly probability evidence and that you could not believe that it was conclusive.

In your final paragraph, you say that I "have probably avoided them [gross problems] in your new edition as surely as you did in the earlier ones." I think that this is both untrue and unfair. What is true, as I think that you will in fairness recognize, is that you and I do not always see the same things as problems. While I can appreciate your frustration that you have been unable to convince me of the importance of some things that I regard as non-issues, it is hardly fair to accuse me of evading issues that I simply do not see as such. Besides, that would be a two-edged sword.

Let me cite a few—out of many—passages in which I (or we, for I have a co-author) have acknowledged difficulties, differing viewpoints, inadequate or missing data, etc.:

p. 62. " . . . there was much unsound biology associated with the biogenetic law . . . ."

p. 96. "Does it [the fossil record] record phylogeny? In part . . . at the species level . . . the picture is considerably less clear."

p. 98. "For C. Patterson, the information content of fossils is too low to rely upon for the reconstruction of phylogenies . . . fossils are to be 'plugged in' to phylogenies based on living animals."

p. 244. "The species question is, then, at once one of the most basic problems of biology and of evolution and one for which no satisfactory answer is available."

p. 344. "As a result, conjecture plays a larger role in diagnosing relationships among phyla than is usual in scientific decision making."

p. 358. " . . . this is an assumption for the proof of which no data are available . . . ."

p. 379. In reference to Chapters 16 and 17: "Thus it is altogether probable that decisive fossil evidence on the problems discussed in these chapters will never be obtained, and these subjects must always remain speculative . . . ."

p. 412. "None of these reasons is conclusive . . . ."

p. 414. "Embryology is not a safe basis for construction of pedigrees . . . ."

p. 422. " . . . the echinoderm theory now has more support than does any other theory of chordate origin, but few would care to claim that it is securely established."

p. 499. "Regarding the factual findings there is no disagreement, but there has been much disagreement regarding their interpretation."

p. 525. "All three schools have been severely criticized by the others . . . the final resolution of these controversies is still in the future."

p. 535. "As a morphological series, this example is undisputed among paleoanthropologists; whether it is also a phylogenetic series is very much disputed."

Previously, you have commended me for such openness to the problems and doubts. Nonetheless, this series of quotations hoists me on my own petard, for the context is not there. However, you can easily get the context, for that is the new edition of *Evolution: Process and Product*. It should be out before you receive this letter, and you may see it before I do, because we are now threatened with a postal strike. If it is not averted by last minute negotiations, delivery of my personal copies may be delayed indefinitely.

In closing, let me just add that we are in agreement that "the truth will out." When it is fully disclosed, I am confident that, on the scientific side, it will confirm the main aspects of evolution; and on the religious side, it will confirm the harmony of Christian revelation with all aspects of science, including evolution. As Teilhard said, research and adoration will converge.

Sincerely yours,

Edward O. Dodson

May 22, 1985

Dear Dr. Dodson:

Thanks for clearing up your position on the Colin Patterson tape transcript. I was, in fact, upset, as you surmised, because I had shipped information to be evaluated by a colleague. Instead of evaluating the evidence I had sent, you began questioning my ethics so that, rather than having had a "bad day" (as we all can have and as you surmised my problem to be), I was rightly concerned over what seemed to be an attempt to dodge the fact that there is deep unrest in many quarters of orthodox evolutionism—something which must disturb you after spending the lion's share of your career teaching and writing about a non-scientific field as if it were in fact science. Now that people like Patterson, Gould, and others (admittedly not creationists but at the same time critical) are beginning to "blow the whistle" on some of the tenets that had been center ground for the neo-Darwinian synthesis, this can in fact be very upsetting. So I forgive you for dodging facts and trying to impugn my ethics—this is a very natural response.

I apologize for suggesting that your book was rigid in areas that you have in fact qualified very well, as your thorough display of quotations demonstrated. I shall in fact try to secure a copy soon for our library (still pulling out of the recession, our college has had limited book funds available). When I do study the text I probably will not find that you have given scientific creationism alternative status with macroevolutionism. Even though you are a brother in Christ, it appears that Teilhard looms larger in your thoughts than Moses. Whereas you take Moses figuratively, I take Teilhard with a grain of sodium chloride and I guess that's where some of the contrast lies between our two religio-philosophical origins concepts. We both respect each other's science (where we have a common agreement on what constitutes real science) and we both respect the other's faith in Christ (although of admittedly different traditions). When it comes to origins, you rather have the opinion (and you are not alone in this misconception) that there is such a structure of origins data supporting evolution—and only evolution—that the word science can be draped over the whole system; I believe that these so-called "scientific data" that "demand" evolution have equal or better fit in a view that you class as religious—and in your mind wrong religion to boot. Probably there can be no synthesis of this point and you will go on fondly hoping that someday Teilhard will be vindicated, and I imagine that when we learn the real facts from Christ the creationists will be closer to actuality than their adversaries. Meanwhile, we can carry out a charitable exchange of ideas and letters (provided the trend doesn't keep us both from doing what we should; note that this letter is a reversal of the J-shaped growth curve our correspondence was taking). Thus, I can realize that, if I ever need the opinion of a "card-carrying" evolutionist, I can bounce some ideas off you and my other correspondent, C. Gordon Winder of the Department of Geology at the University of Western Ontario. Have you heard from this chap? He holds to wholesale evolutionism philosophically in conjunction with a Biblical theology and corresponds as well. I enclose some material of his for your file. He has a type of Biblical theistic evolutionism that he wants Canada to adopt as an educational compromise between evolution and creation. Like so many evolutionists, however, he wants this to be done to the exclusion of the views I represent on origins. Evolutionists want to indoctrinate youngsters in the public schools to the exclusion of other viable origins philosophies (and at taxpayers' expense, no less). But as with you, there has been an attempt by both Winder and me to carry on continued dialogue and I believe that this is wholesome in the interest of science and Christianity—fields we all profess to straddle.

I hope your postal strike didn't cause much trouble and that your summer goes well. I am traveling now, visiting relatives in Illinois, Ohio, New York, Mississippi, then home.

Best regards,

G. Howe

July 16, 1985

Dear Dr. Howe:

I'm sorry that I gave the impression that I was criticizing you on ethical grounds. That was not my intention at all, so I must have written very badly.

You asked whether I had heard from Dr. C. Gordon Winder. Yes, but only indirectly. He wrote to our Dean of Graduate Studies, asking him to endorse his Positive Policy and to send that endorsement to the Minister of Education for Ontario. The Dean asked me to read Winder's proposal and to advise him. As you know, Winder believes that evolution is included in the Bible, but that this can be established only orally (via tapes that Winder sells), not by reading specified texts. I told the Dean that I was doubtful whether anything other than music could be understood only by ear, and that I could not believe that creationists would agree to Winder's Positive Policy, as he seems to think they should. I therefore recommended that he send Winder a courteous but non-committal reply. This he did.

You also said that "Teilhard looms larger in your thoughts than Moses." I wouldn't really say that. I think of Teilhard as supplementary to Moses rather than as contradictory. Moses wrote for a pre-scientific people for whom a scientific explanation would have been unintelligible. Teilhard wrote for people who have been dominated by scientifically oriented culture, and for whom the supposed contradictions of science and of religious faith have often been accepted as proof that religion is outmoded. Every practising scientist who is also a practising Christian therefore serves an apostolate of great importance in the modern world. Because of his importance in both religion and science, Teilhard has especial importance as an apostle to today's scientifically oriented society. I do not doubt that Moses rejoices in the Teilhardian complement to his own work.

You also said with respect to my book that "I probably will not find that you have given scientific creationism alternative status with macroevolutionism." You are right if you mean equal status. I have stated that scientific creationism is an alternative preferred by creationists, and that data interpreted in my book as evidence of evolution are interpreted by creationists as evidence of creation on a common plan. Also, I have given references to several books that defend scientific creationism. Thus, I have tried to be fair, but I have not tried to hide the fact that I believe that much of evolutionary biology is scientifically sound (of course, there is some unsound work in any discipline whatever).

Finally, I would like to refer back to your preceding letter, in which you stated rather emphatically that evolutionists are religionists. You may be surprised that we are in at least partial agreement. Anything whatever can be perverted to form the basis of a false religion. Why not evolution? Nonetheless, the converse is not true: an evolutionary biologist may follow his profession on a strictly scientific basis, while satisfying his religious needs in other ways. I know that evolution is not my religion, nor that of my co-author, my son Peter. I know that Dobzhansky was a devout Christian. For all of us, our religion is Christianity, but our scientific experience has convinced us that He created by an evolutionary process.

Enjoy your summer travels and visits!

Sincerely yours,

Edward O. Dodson

August 6, 1985

Dear Dr. Howe:

L et me return again to your last letter. You said that you had sent me, as a colleague, a report for evaluation, a report indicating deep unrest among evolutionists. You were disappointed because, instead of evaluating it, I had merely brought up several biochemists who "chant the party lines."

That letter to which you were responding must have been one of my poorest, because I failed completely to get across the evaluation that I was attempting. My principal point was that I am always disappointed when an expert in one field bases his argument on a different field in which he has no particular expertise. Patterson is an outstanding paleontologist and taxonomist, yet he based his argument on biochemistry. I found that transcript largely unintelligible, and he himself said that it "was badly garbled in places." As to biochemists who "chant the party lines," this can hardly apply to such scientists as W. M. Fitch, E. Margoliash, and Margaret Dayhoff. These are the leaders whom others may follow. The only biochemist I know of who does not interpret his data in an evolutionary frame of reference is Duane Gish, and he seems to prefer to write about paleontology. I regard this as evaluation, even if along lines different from those that you had anticipated.

Whatever else may have been garbled, it is clear that Patterson did show "deep unrest." I don't think that this is true of many evolutionary biologists, and I would think it more significant if he related it to his own field of expertise. Actually, in his letter to me, he did. He said that he did not consider it helpful to treat evolution as axiomatic in taxonomy—and he does have professional standing in taxonomy. I told you that I agree with him—I don't believe that evolution should be treated as axiomatic in any field. It is a proposition to be tested and proved or disproved. That, too, is evaluation, perhaps closer to your expectations.

As to Gould, you already know that I am not among his admirers but, as I told you long ago, I am rather sympathetic to his ideas about punctuated equilibrium, because they are closely related to the ideas of my old teacher, Richard Goldschmidt. My first book on evolution, way back in 1952, was criticized partly because it was open to this viewpoint at a time when neo-Darwinism was new and strongly ascendant. I regarded Goldschmidt's dissent as healthful in a very actively developing science in which there were major unsolved problems. Today, I see punctuated equilibrium in very much the same light. Although I have never been among those who regard neo-Darwinism as the answer to all evolutionary problems, I think that the neo-Darwinian synthesis is stronger today than it was when I first wrote about it.

I still do not believe that all of the answers are in, and I think that it is a mistake to try to explain evolution on a single, fairly simple basis. There may be room for both neo-Darwinism and punctuated equilibrium, or it may prove necessary to replace both as new research clarifies some of the currently unsolved problems.

Finally, you say that you think that the whole truth, when we learn it from Christ, will be closer to the creationist viewpoint. Unfortunately, we will both have to await the resurrection for that final resolution of our differences. Meanwhile, I am as confident as you are.

I had hoped that this would all go on one page, but unfortunately I just missed. I hope that I have at least been clear this time.

Sincerely yours,

Edward O. Dodson

August 18, 1985

Dear Dr. Dodson:

In your last two letters, which were of high quality and a balanced vision, you have allayed my fears that you were possibly attempting to center on supposed ethical criticisms of Sunderland and me while missing the point of Patterson's thrust. You have admirably summarized our areas of agreement and I support your assertion that we will both have to await the resurrection to sort out all of the threads of difference which occur between our respective fabrics of scientific apologetics. The wonderful aspect of that event, as well, will be that neither of us will have the "I told you so" attitude when the other is shown to err in one tenet or another, as we shall be so taken up with the presence and charisma of this God-man who bore our sins that we will be free at last from what the great apostle Paul called "the old man" or "the old nature."

Thus, although we received the new man or new nature upon our profession of faith in Christ, this old nature persists in all true believers no matter how seriously they attempt to be filled with the Holy Spirit or to work for God. Because of this there will always be division between born-again Catholics, born-again Baptists, and born-again Pentecostals. The *old* man in each prevents proper surrender of heretical views *each* one holds. So I am no great champion of ecumenism, as it leads to mere "liberalism" and other apostate nonsense. In some cases it is the stupidity of our old nature, and in other cases it's simple bigotry.

Because of this, as well, Satan will always have ammunition to use against Christians in his attempt to make them stumble and to dissuade non-believers from trusting Jesus. Our enemy will always be able to point toward materialistic ministers in the "electronic church" or to priests and nuns who bring disgrace on the name of their Lord in various ways!

But ultimately and in His wisdom, the Creator will judge each person regarding the *sine qua non* of salvation which lies in confession of Christ as Son of God and personal savior. Those *outside* such faith will face degrees of punishment.

We will probably find no more use dwelling on the subject in our correspondence, as I do not expect you and other evolutionists who are far less gentlemanly or cordial than yourself to openly admit that "origins" is different from "science" and that creationism is no more "religious" and no less "scientific" than any or all of the various evolutionary speculations. Since you will dodge *any* logic I use to support this (what to me seems) *obvious* fact, there is little use in our pursuance of origins much further in our letters, as you will nimbly but cordially move into a kind of Jesuit circuitry that ends up calling white black. Mind you, you are not the *only* evolutionist with such warped and hopelessly slanted usage of the word "science." I also agree that you have "tried" to be fair in your book—you have tried as hard as anyone can try who persists in clothing origins models like evolutionism with the moniker of "science." Let's let the matter *rest*, as we are most likely permanently *separated* on what is "science" and what is not. And don't be smug just because hundreds of mindless colleagues (philosophically "mindless") happen to agree with your distorted opinions.

We could far better confine our comments to theology, politics, pleasantries, and even Christian fellowship across the chasm of denominational blunderings. I shall send reprints of my new papers as they appear and will appreciate it if you do the same. Hope my letter finds you enjoying August and resting in God's good provisions for physical and spiritual life.

Best regards,

George F. Howe

October 4, 1985

Dear Dr. Howe:

In your letter of August 18, you suggested it might not be useful to continue our correspondence on the subject of origins. I am inclined to agree with you. We have probably both said most of what we have to say on the subject, and neither of us is likely to change his opinions.

One of my sons, who has read all of our correspondence, has suggested that we publish it. He believes that it will appeal to three constituencies: other fundamentalists, who will be interested in your response to the evolutionary challenge; other evolutionary biologists, who would be interested in my response to the fundamentalist arguments; and, finally, members of the neutral public, who would be interested in reading both sides of an issue that has been repeatedly brought before legislatures and courts in recent years. I think that he may be right about this. If you agree, I would be glad to do the work of preparing it for publication (retyping, double-spaced, with wide margins). For the present, however, I am teaching this semester, and I no longer have the stamina for steady, long-continued work. After the preparation of the manuscript, it would be necessary to try to get a publisher to take it. What do you think?

I am sure that you are right that there will be no "I told you so" attitude in heaven. We will all rejoice in the understanding of the whole truth and especially in the immediate presence of the Blessed Trinity.

I agree with you that the species of ecumenism that seeks a least common denominator is not useful, but ecumenism doesn't have to be that. The basic fact here, I think, is the prayer of Our Lord "that they may all be one . . . so that the world may believe that you sent me." It is impossible that the prayer of Christ should not be fulfilled, and that implies ecumenism, although not necessarily any specific ecumenical organization. Some aspects of ecumenism have had useful results. For example, high-level talks between Catholics and Lutherans have resulted in agreement on the issues that led to the Reformation, including agreement that the minor issues that remain unresolved are insufficient to justify continued separation. This does not mean, of course, that reunion will follow immediately. Four hundred years of schism cannot be healed that quickly. But the healing process is well under way, and I think that we can be sure that it will be completed. Similar talks between Catholics and Anglicans (= Episcopalians in the U.S.) have also gone far and with much success.

You say that I "will dodge *any* logic I use to support this . . . *obvious* fact . . . as you will nimbly but cordially move into a kind of Jesuit circuitry that ends up calling white black." To this, I will just make two comments. First, to me evolution is as obvious as is creationism to you. And second, I think that the overwhelming majority of our professional colleagues would consider that it is not I, but yourself, who has evaded logic and who is burdened with "distorted opinions." You caution me not to be smug because of the support of "hundreds of mindless colleagues." This is a rather harsh judgment on a large number of highly productive scientists. It is also the *ad hominem* argument against which you once cautioned me. Aside from that, you are, of course, right that majorities are not necessarily right. But neither are they necessarily wrong; nor are minorities, even very dedicated and conscientious minorities, necessarily right. So what were you saying about smugness?

So we leave our long discussion of origins. I await with great interest your reaction to the suggestion that we publish our correspondence on origins.

Sincerely yours,

Edward O. Dodson

Notes

1. Further information about most of the people mentioned in these letters can be found in Appendix 1.
2. Dr. Vladykov died on January 15, 1986, after a very long career.
3. All Biblical texts not quoted in full in the letters are reprinted, in the order in which they appear in the Bible, in Appendix 2. Where whole chapters are cited (other than Genesis 1 and 2), we must ask the reader to refer to his own Bible.
4. This book was published in 1984 as *The Phenomenon of Man Revisited: A Biological Viewpoint on Teilhard de Chardin* (Columbia University Press, New York).
5. The National Association of Biology Teachers (NABT) publishes *The American Biology Teacher*.
6. Note that comments by Howe were sent to Dodson along the margin of the two previous letters, as follows:

   Although scientific certainty is almost non-existent, there is a matter of degree involved such that there exists a quantum jump between science and what should be called origins. Evolutionists realize this and the sad fact is they refuse to admit the same.

   In requesting evidence that would really "demand" evolution, I mean demand in the same sense that we use the word in biological laboratory research. Thus, origins differs from real science because the latter emerges as the *best* among *repeatable* verifiable experiments supporting an hypothesis.

   Am I sure that my own convictions have not overridden my scientific judgment? Yes, because I have said right along that origins lies largely outside science.   G.F.H.

   It is gratuitous for G.F.H. to state that evolutionary biologists agree with him and refuse to admit it. As I have said elsewhere in this correspondence, we are well aware that many aspects of macroevolutionary science are less secure than is microevolutionary science. There is good assurance, however, about some aspects of macroevolution, and I do not believe that the "quantum jump" of which he speaks is genuine.

   Second, as the evidence for evolution has convinced the overwhelming majority of working biologists, it is fair to conclude that this evidence meets his criterion of demanding evolution "in the sense that we use the word in biological laboratory research."

   Finally, the fact that he has said "right along" that "origins lies largely outside science" proves that he has been consistent, but it has no bearing on whether he has allowed his convictions to overrule his scientific judgment.   E.O.D.

7. A news item concerning controversy at the Southern Baptist Convention.
8. In commenting on this discussion of 1 Corinthians 11:27–29, Dr. Howe discussed those aspects of this passage on which we are agreed. He does not seem to have addressed verse 29: "For he who eats and drinks unworthily, *without distinguishing the body*, eats and drinks judgment to himself." This verse would seem to be unfavorable to a figurative interpretation of the sacrament.   E.O.D.

   While this verse would suggest to E.O.D. that a figurative interpretation of the sacrament is not acceptable, I would assert that the writer (the apostle Paul) here also deals with those who flippantly misuse this important symbol of Christ's body.   G.F.H.

9. *Drosophila* is a genus of fruit flies, the small flies that flit about fresh fruit in the summer. Among the many species of this large genus, *D. pseudoobscura* was long ago described from the southwestern U.S. It is called *pseudo*obscura because it closely resembles an Old World species, *D. obscura.* Researchers who investigated this species soon found that it included two subgroups that were very difficult to distinguish by appearance; nonetheless, they were separated by a sterility barrier. They were first designated as *D. ps.* A and B, but it was finally decided that they were closely similar species (sibling species). Race A bears the original name, and race B is now called *D. persimilis.* Finally, a third species, *D. miranda*, is also quite similar. All have giant chromosomes in the salivary glands of their larvae, and changes in the patterns of these giant chromosomes can be traced through the series, thus giving evolutionary biologists confidence in the details of relationships in the series.

Appendix 1
Names Appearing in the Letters

Isaac Asimov (1920–). American biochemist, and prolific writer of both science and science fiction.

Winona C. Barker (1938–). American biochemist who has published important work on the evolution of proteins.

Francis Crick (1916–). One of the principal investigators of the structure of DNA, for which he received a Nobel prize.

Margaret O. Dayhoff (1925–1983). American biochemist, and a leader in research on protein phylogenies.

Henri de Lubac (1896–). French Jesuit priest and long a friend of Teilhard de Chardin; since 1983, Henri Cardinal de Lubac.

Theodosius Dobzhansky (1900–1975). Russian-American geneticist, a leading innovator in evolutionary research, and the principal architect of modern evolutionary synthesis. Often called the Dean of modern evolutionary biologists.

R. F. Doolittle (1931–). American biochemist who has done extensive work on molecular phylogenies.

R. A. Fisher (1890–1962). British statistician and geneticist, and one of the principal founders of modern statistics and mathematical genetics.

W. M. Fitch (1929–). American biochemist, and one of the first (with Margoliash) to construct phylogenies based on sequences of amino acids in proteins.

S. W. Fox (1912–). American biochemist with research interests on the origin of life.

Douglas Futuyma (1942–). Editor of *Evolution*, and author of a highly regarded text on evolution.

Duane Gish (1921–). American biochemist, prolific writer on scientific creationism, and Associate Director of the Institute for Creation Research.

Richard B. Goldschmidt (1878–1958). A distinguished German-American geneticist, and champion of minority ideas in evolutionary biology.

Stephen Jay Gould (1941–). American biologist–paleontologist–geologist, and prolific writer of popular evolutionary science.

John C. Greene (1917–). American historian of science who has written much about evolution.

J.B.S. Haldane (1892–1964). English biologist whose wide-ranging research includes important work on the mathematical basis of evolutionary theory.

Lancelot Hogben (1895–1975). English physiologist and mathematical geneticist.

Fred Hoyle (1915–). English astronomer and cosmologist, and advocate of the origin of life in outer space.

Carl Hubbs (1894–1981). American zoologist, and an outstanding authority on North American fishes.

Julian Huxley (1887–1975). British evolutionary biologist and prolific author.

G. A. Kerkut. Contemporary British zoologist, and author of a book on the problems of evolutionary biology, *Implications of Evolution* (1960).

R. E. Leakey (1944–). Director of the National Museum of Kenya, and an important student of human evolution, as were both his parents, Louis and Mary Leakey.

Sir Charles Lyell (1797–1875). Considered one of the founders of modern geology, although educated as a lawyer.

E. Margoliash (1920–). American biochemist who collaborated with Fitch to construct the first phylogenies based on the sequences of amino acids in specific proteins.

Gregor Mendel (1822–1884). Austrian monk whose experiments on plant hybridization resulted in the origin of the science of genetics.

John N. Moore (1920–). American biologist and a leading creationist.

Henry M. Morris (1918–). American hydraulic engineer, and Director of the Institute for Creation Research.

John A. O'Brien (1893–1980). American priest and author-in-residence at the University of Notre Dame for many years. Prolific writer who published much on science and religion, and saw no necessary conflict between evolution and faith.

Blaise Pascal (1623–1662). French mathematician, philosopher, and writer on spiritual subjects.

Colin Patterson. Contemporary English paleontologist and taxonomist, and an important member of the staff of the British Museum (Natural History).

Linus Pauling (1901–). American chemist and physicist, and winner of *two* Nobel prizes.

Karl Popper (1902–). Important philosopher of science, who was born and educated in Vienna, but who moved to England early in his career in response to the Nazi threat.

Alfred S. Romer (1894–1973). American paleontologist whose books have fired the evolutionary interests of many students.

Carl Sagan (1934–). American astronomer, specialist on planetary sciences, and prolific writer of popular science.

George Gaylord Simpson (1902–1984). American paleontologist, and an outstanding authority on the evolution of mammals.

Grafton E. Smith (1871–1937). Australian anatomist, later at Manchester and London, and a suspect in the Piltdown fraud.

William Smith (1769–1839). English engineer who, while building canals, worked out the principles of relative dating of geological strata.

W. J. Sollas (1849–1936). English geologist and anthropologist, and a prime suspect in the Piltdown fraud.

W. D. Stansfield (1930–). American biologist, and author of a widely used text on evolution.

G. Ledyard Stebbins (1906–). American evolutionary botanist, and an authority on polyploidy and plant development from an evolutionary viewpoint.

Pierre Teilhard de Chardin (1881–1955). French Jesuit priest and paleontologist, and author of *The Phenomenon of Man*, a synthesis of his faith as a priest and his evolutionary science as a paleontologist.

Karl Ernst von Baer (1792–1876). German embryologist who proposed important principles for the interpretation of comparative embryology.

N. C. Wickramasinghe (1939–). Mathematician; colleague of, and co-author with, Hoyle.

Appendix 2
Biblical References

The sources of Biblical quotations are identified by initials, as follows:

CCD   Confraternity of Christian Doctrine edition of the New Testament, a revision of the Challoner–Rheims version. St. Anthony Guild Press. Paterson, New Jersey. 1941.

CR   Challoner–Rheims version. Hawthorn Books. New York. 1958.

GNMM   Good News for Modern Man. The New Testament in Today's English Version. American Bible Society. New York. 1971.

NASB   New American Standard Bible. Holman Bible Publishers. Nashville, Tennessee. © 1977, The Lockman Foundation. Used by permission. (All of Dr. Howe's quotes are from this version.)

Genesis 1. In the beginning God created the heavens and the earth.   2. And the earth was formless and void, and darkness was over the surface of the deep; and the Spirit of God was moving over the surface of the waters.   3. Then God said, "Let there be light"; and there was light.   4. And God saw that the light was good; and God separated the light from the darkness.   5. And God called the light day, and the darkness He called night. And there was evening and there was morning, one day.

6. Then God said, "Let there be an expanse in the midst of the waters, and let it separate the waters from the waters."   7. And God made the expanse, and separated the waters which were below the expanse from the waters which were above the expanse; and it was so.   8. And God called the expanse heaven. And there was evening and there was morning, a second day.

9. Then God said, "Let the waters below the heavens be gathered into one place, and let the dry land appear"; and it was so.   10. And God called the dry land earth, and the gathering of the waters He called seas; and God saw that it was good.   11. Then God said, "Let the earth sprout vegetation, plants yielding seed, *and* fruit trees bearing fruit after their kind, with seed in them, on the earth"; and it was so.   12. And the earth brought forth vegetation, plants yielding seed after their kind, and trees bearing fruit, with seed in them, after their kind; and God saw that it was good.   13. And there was evening and there was morning, a third day.

14. Then God said, "Let there be lights in the expanse of the heavens to separate the day from the night, and let them be for signs, and for seasons, and for days and years;   15. and let them be for lights in the expanse of the

heavens to give light on the earth"; and it was so.   16. And God made the two great lights, the greater light to govern the day, and the lesser light to govern the night; *He made* the stars also.   17. And God placed them in the expanse of the heavens to give light on the earth,   18. and to govern the day and the night, and to separate the light from the darkness; and God saw that it was good.   19. And there was evening and there was morning, a fourth day.

20. Then God said, "Let the waters teem with swarms of living creatures, and let birds fly above the earth in the open expanse of the heavens."   21. And God created the great sea monsters, and every living creature that moves, with which the waters swarmed after their kind, and every winged bird after its kind; and God saw that it was good.   22. And God blessed them, saying, "Be fruitful and multiply, and fill the waters in the seas, and let birds multiply on the earth."   23. And there was evening and there was morning, a fifth day.

24. Then God said, "Let the earth bring forth living creatures after their kind: cattle and creeping things and beasts of the earth after their kind"; and it was so.   25. And God made the beasts of the earth after their kind, and the cattle after their kind, and everything that creeps on the ground after its kind; and God saw that it was good.   26. Then God said, "Let Us make man in Our image, according to Our likeness; and let them rule over the fish of the sea and over the birds of the sky and over the cattle and over all the earth, and over every creeping thing that creeps on the earth."   27. And God created man in His own image, in the image of God He created him; male and female He created them.   28. And God blessed them; and God said to them, "Be fruitful and multiply, and fill the earth, and subdue it; and rule over the fish of the sea and over the birds of the sky, and over every living thing that moves on the earth."   29. Then God said, "Behold, I have given you every plant yielding seed that is on the surface of all the earth, and every tree which has fruit yielding seed; it shall be food for you;   30. and to every beast of the earth and to every bird of the sky and to every thing that moves on the earth which has life, *I have given* every green plant for food"; and it was so.   31. And God saw all that He had made, and behold, it was very good. And there was evening and there was morning, the sixth day.

Genesis 2. Thus the heavens and the earth were completed, and all their hosts.   2. And by the seventh day God completed His work which He had done; and He rested on the seventh day from all His work which He had done.   3. Then God blessed the seventh day and sanctified it, because in it He rested from all His work which God had created and made.

4. This is the account of the heavens and the earth when they were created, in the day that the LORD God made earth and heaven.   5. Now no shrub of the field was yet in the earth, and no plant of the field had yet sprouted, for the LORD God had not sent rain upon the earth; and there was no man to cultivate the ground.   6. But a mist used to rise from the earth and water the whole surface of the ground.   7. Then the LORD God formed

man of dust from the ground, and breathed into his nostrils the breath of life; and man became a living being.   8. And the LORD God planted a garden toward the east, in Eden; and there He placed the man whom He had formed.   9. And out of the ground the LORD God caused to grow every tree that is pleasing to the sight and good for food; the tree of life also in the midst of the garden, and the tree of the knowledge of good and evil.

10. Now a river flowed out of Eden to water the garden; and from there it divided and became four rivers.   11. The name of the first is Pishon; it flows around the whole land of Havilah, where there is gold.   12. And the gold of that land is good; the bdellium and the onyx stone are there.   13. And the name of the second river is Gihon; it flows around the whole land of Cush.   14. And the name of the third river is Tigris; it flows east of Assyria. And the fourth river is the Euphrates.   15. Then the LORD God took the man and put him into the garden of Eden to cultivate it and keep it.   16. And the LORD God commanded the man, saying, "From any tree of the garden you may eat freely;   17. but from the tree of the knowledge of good and evil you shall not eat, for in the day that you eat from it you shall surely die."

18. Then the LORD God said, "It is not good for the man to be alone; I will make him a helper suitable for him."   19. And out of the ground the LORD God formed every beast of the field and every bird of the sky, and brought *them* to the man to see what he would call them; and whatever the man called a living creature, that was its name.   20. And the man gave names to all the cattle, and to the birds of the sky, and to every beast of the field, but for Adam there was not found a helper suitable for him.   21. So the LORD God caused a deep sleep to fall upon the man, and he slept; then He took one of his ribs, and closed up the flesh at that place.   22. And the LORD God fashioned into a woman the rib which He had taken from the man, and brought her to the man.   23. And the man said,

> "This is now bone of my bones,
> And flesh of my flesh;
> She shall be called Woman,
> Because she was taken out of
> Man."

24. For this cause a man shall leave his father and his mother, and shall cleave to his wife; and they shall become one flesh.   25. And the man and his wife were both naked and were not ashamed.   (NASB)

Exodus 20:11. For in six days the Lord made heaven and earth, and the sea, and all things that are in them, and rested on the seventh day: therefore the Lord blessed the seventh day, and sanctified it.   (CR)

Leviticus 11:4, 6, 13, 19. But whatsoever cheweth indeed the cud, and hath a hoof, but divideth it not, as the camel, and others, that you shall not eat, but shall reckon it among the unclean.   6. The hare also: for that too cheweth the cud but divideth not the hoof.   13. Of birds these are they which you must not eat.   19. . . . and the bat.   (CR)

Matthew 7:3–5. "Why, then, do you look at the speck in your brother's eye, and pay no attention to the log in your own eye?   4. How dare you say to your brother, 'Please, let me take the speck out of your eye,' when you have a log in your own eye?   5. You hypocrite! Take the log out of your own eye first, and then you will be able to see and take the speck out of your brother's eye."   (GNMM)

Matthew 7:21. "Not everyone who calls me 'Lord, Lord,' will enter into the Kingdom of heaven, but only those who do what my Father in heaven wants them to do."   (GNMM)

Matthew 10:22. And you will be hated by all for my name's sake; but he who has persevered to the end will be saved.   (CCD)

Matthew 16:16–19. Simon Peter answered, "You are the Messiah, the Son of the living God."
17. "Good for you, Simon, son of John!" answered Jesus. "Because this truth did not come to you from any human being, but it was given to you directly by my Father in heaven.   18. And so I tell you: you are a rock, Peter, and on this rock foundation I will build my church, which not even death will be able to overcome.   19. I will give you the keys of the Kingdom of heaven; what you prohibit on earth will be prohibited in heaven; what you permit on earth will be permitted in heaven."   (GNMM)

Matthew 26:26–29. And while they were at supper, Jesus took bread, and blessed and broke, and gave it to his disciples, and said, "Take and eat; this is my body."   27. And taking a cup, he gave thanks and gave it to them, saying, "All of you drink of this;   28. for this is my blood of the new covenant, which is being shed for many unto the forgiveness of sins.   29. But I say to you, I will drink henceforth of this fruit of the vine, until that day when I shall drink it new with you in the kingdom of my Father."   (CCD)

Mark 14:22–25. And while they were eating, Jesus took bread, and blessing it, he broke and gave it to them, and said, "Take; this is my body."   23. And taking a cup and giving thanks, he gave it to them, and they all drank of it;   24. and he said to them, "This is my blood of the new covenant, which is being shed for many.   25. Amen I say to you, that I will drink no more of the fruit of the vine, until that day when I shall drink it new in the kingdom of God."   (CCD)

Luke 5:3–11. Jesus got into one of the boats—it belonged to Simon— and asked him to push off a little from the shore. Jesus sat in the boat and taught the crowd.
4. When he had finished speaking, he said to Simon, "Push the boat out further into the deep water, and you and your partners let your nets down for a catch."

5. "Master," Simon answered, "we worked hard all night long and caught nothing. But if you say so, I will let down the nets."
6. They let the nets down and caught such a large number of fish that the nets were about to break.   7. So they motioned to their partners in the other boats to come and help them. They came and filled both boats so full of fish that they were about to sink.   8. When Simon Peter saw what had happened, he fell on his knees before Jesus and said, "Go away from me, Lord! I am a sinful man!"
9. He and the others with him were all amazed at the large number of fish they had caught.   10. The same was true of Simon's partners, James and John, the sons of Zebedee. Jesus said to Simon, "Don't be afraid; from now on you will be catching men."
11. They pulled the boats on the beach, left everything, and followed Jesus.   (GNMM)

Luke 10:16. "He who hears you, hears me; and he who rejects you, rejects me; and he who rejects me, rejects him who sent me."   (CCD)

Luke 22:19–20. And having taken bread, he gave thanks and broke, and gave it to them, saying, "This is my body, which is being given for you; do this in remembrance of me."   20. In like manner he took also the cup after the supper, saying, "This cup is the new covenant in my blood, which shall be shed for you."   (CCD)

Luke 22:32. "But I have prayed for you, Simon, that your faith will not fail. And when you turn back to me, you must strengthen your brothers."   (GNMM)

Luke 24:49. And I myself will send upon you what my Father has promised. But you must wait in the city until the power from above comes down upon you.   (GNMM)

John 3:16. For God so loved the world, that He gave His only begotten Son, that whoever believes in Him should not perish, but have eternal life.   (NASB)

John 6:30–69. They therefore said to him, "What sign, then, dost thou, that we may see and believe thee? What work dost thou perform?   31. Our fathers ate manna in the desert, even as it is written,
    'Bread from heaven he gave them to eat.'"
32. Jesus then said to them, "Amen, amen, I say to you, Moses did not give you the bread from heaven, but my Father gives you the true bread from heaven.   33. For the bread of God is that which comes down from heaven and gives life to the world."
34. They therefore said to him, "Lord, give us always this bread."

35. But Jesus said to them, "I am the bread of life. He who comes to me shall not hunger, and he who believes in me shall never thirst. 36. But I have told you that you have seen me and you do not believe. 37. All that the Father gives to me shall come to me, and him who comes to me I will not cast out. 38. For I have come down from heaven, not to do my own will, but the will of him who sent me. 39. Now this is the will of him who sent me, the Father, that I should lose nothing of what he has given me, but that I should raise it up on the last day. 40. For this is the will of my Father who sent me, that whoever beholds the Son, and believes in him, shall have everlasting life, and I will raise him up on the last day."

41. The Jews therefore murmured about him because he had said, "I am the bread that has come down from heaven." 42. And they kept saying, "Is this not Jesus the son of Joseph, whose father and mother we know? How, then, does he say, 'I have come down from heaven'?"

43. In answer therefore Jesus said to them, "Do not murmur among yourselves. 44. No one can come to me unless the Father who sent me draws him, and I will raise him up on the last day. 45. It is written in the prophets,
    'And they shall all be taught of God.'
Everyone who has listened to the Father, and has learned, comes to me; 46. not that anyone has seen the Father except him who is from God, he has seen the Father. 47. Amen, amen, I say to you, he who believes in me has life everlasting.

48. I am the bread of life. 49. Your fathers ate the manna in the desert, and have died. 50. This is the bread that comes down from heaven, so that if anyone eat it he will not die. 51. I am the living bread that has come down from heaven. If anyone eat of this bread he shall live forever; and the bread that I will give is my flesh for the life of the world."

52. The Jews on that account argued with one another, saying, "How can this man give us his flesh to eat?"

53. Jesus therefore said to them, "Amen, amen, I say to you, unless you eat the flesh of the Son of Man, and drink his blood, you shall not have life in you. 54. He who eats my flesh and drinks my blood has life everlasting and I will raise him up on the last day. 55. For my flesh is food indeed, and my blood is drink indeed. 56. He who eats my flesh, and drinks my blood, abides in me and I in him. 57. As the living Father has sent me, and as I live because of the Father, so he who eats me, he also shall live because of me.

58. This is the bread that has come down from heaven; not as your fathers ate the manna and died. He who eats this bread shall live forever."

59. These things he said when teaching in the synagogue at Capharnum.

60. Many of his disciples therefore, when they heard this, said, "This is a hard saying. Who can listen to it?" 61. But Jesus, knowing in himself that his disciples were murmuring at this, said to them, "Does this scandalize you? 62. What then if you should see the Son of Man ascending where he was before? 63. It is the spirit that gives life; the flesh profits nothing. The words that I have spoken to you are spirit and life. 64. But there are some

among you who do not believe." For Jesus knew from the beginning who they were who did not believe, and who it was who should betray him.

65. And he said, "This is why I have said to you, 'No one can come to me unless he is enabled to do so by my Father.'"   66. From this time many of his disciples turned back and no longer went about with him.

67. Jesus therefore said to the twelve, "Do you also wish to go away?"   68. Simon Peter therefore answered, "Lord, to whom shall we go? Thou hast the words of everlasting life,   69. and we have come to believe and to know that thou art the Christ, the Son of God."   (CCD)

John 6:56. He who eats My flesh and drinks My blood abides in Me and I in him.   (NASB)

John 14:26. But the Advocate, the Holy Spirit, whom the Father will send in my name, he will teach you all things, and bring to your mind whatever I have said to you.   (CCD)

John 21:15–19. After they had eaten, Jesus said to Simon Peter, "Simon, son of John, do you love me more than these?"

"Yes, Lord," he answered, "you know that I love you."

Jesus said to him, "Take care of my lambs."   16. A second time Jesus said to him, "Simon, son of John, do you love me?"

"Yes, Lord," he answered, "you know that I love you."

Jesus said to him, "Take care of my sheep."   17. A third time Jesus said, "Simon, son of John, do you love me?"

Peter became sad because Jesus asked him the third time, "Do you love me?" and said to him, "Lord, you know everything; you know that I love you!"

Jesus said to him, "Take care of my sheep.   18. I tell you the truth: When you were young you used to fasten your belt and go anywhere you wanted to; but when you are old you will stretch out your hands and someone else will tie them and take you where you don't want to go."   19. (In saying this Jesus was indicating the way in which Peter would die and bring glory to God.) Then Jesus said to him, "Follow me!"   (GNMM)

John 21:25. And there are also many other things which Jesus did, which if they were written in detail, I suppose that even the world itself would not contain the books which were written.   (NASB)

Acts 5:15. As a result of what the apostles were doing, the sick people were carried out in the streets and placed on beds and mats so that, when Peter walked by, at least his shadow might fall on some of them.   (GNMM)

Romans 5:12. Sin came into the world through one man, and his sin brought death with it. As a result, death spread to the whole human race, because all men sinned.   (GNMM)

Romans 10:9–10. . . . that if you confess with your mouth Jesus as Lord, and believe in your heart that God raised Him from the dead, you shall be saved;   10. for with the heart man believes, resulting in righteousness, and with the mouth he confesses, resulting in salvation.   (NASB)

Romans 11:22. Here we see how kind and how severe God is. He is severe toward those who have fallen, but kind to you—if you continue in his kindness; but if you do not, you will be broken off.   (GNMM)

1 Corinthians 3:10–14. Using the gift that God gave me, I did the work of an expert builder and laid the foundation, and another man is building on it. But each one must be careful how he builds.   11. For God has already placed Jesus Christ as the one and only foundation, and no other foundation can be laid.   12. Some will use gold, or silver, or precious stones in building on the foundation; others will use wood, or grass, or straw.   13. And the quality of each man's work will be seen when the day of Christ exposes it. For that day's fire will reveal every man's work; the fire will test and show its real quality.   14. If what a man built on the foundation survives the fire, he will receive a reward.   (GNMM)

1 Corinthians 10:16–17. The cup of blessing for which we give thanks to God: do we not share in the blood of Christ when we drink from this cup? And the bread we break: do we not share in the body of Christ when we eat this bread?   17. Because there is the one bread, all of us, though many, are one body, because we all share the same loaf.   (GNMM)

1 Corinthians 11:23–29. For I myself have received from the Lord (what I also delivered to you), that the Lord Jesus, on the night in which he was betrayed, took bread,   24. and giving thanks broke, and said, "This is my body which shall be given up for you; do this in remembrance of me."   25. In like manner also the cup, after he had supped, saying, "This cup is the new covenant in my blood; do this as often as you drink it, in remembrance of me.   26. For as often as you shall eat this bread and drink the cup, you proclaim the death of the Lord, until he comes."   27. Therefore whoever eats this bread or drinks the cup of the Lord unworthily, will be guilty of the body and blood of the Lord.   28. But let a man prove himself, and so let him eat of that bread and drink of the cup;   29. for he who eats and drinks unworthily, without distinguishing the body, eats and drinks judgment to himself.   (CCD)

1 Corinthians 11:27–29. Therefore whoever eats the bread or drinks the cup of the Lord in an unworthy manner, shall be guilty of the body and blood of the Lord.   28. But let a man examine himself, and so let him eat the bread and drink the cup.   29. For he who eats and drinks, eats and drinks judgment to himself, if he does not judge the body rightly.   (NASB)

[Notice that the differences between these translations of verses 27–29 are mostly trivial, but the difference between "if he does not judge the body rightly" and "without distinguishing the body" is critical. My own reading of the original Greek supports the latter translation. E.O.D.]

1 Corinthians 15:5. . . . that he appeared to Peter, and then to all twelve apostles.   (GNMM)

Galatians 1:18. Then after three years I went to Jerusalem to see Peter, and I remained with him fifteen days.   (CCD)

Ephesians 3:20. You are built upon the foundation of the apostles and prophets with Christ Jesus himself as the chief corner stone.   (CCD)

Ephesians 5:32. There is a great truth revealed in this scripture, and I understand it applies to Christ and the church.   (GNMM)

1 Peter 2:5. . . . You also, as living stones, are being built up as a spiritual house for a holy priesthood, to offer up spiritual sacrifices acceptable to God through Jesus Christ.   (NASB)

1 Peter 2:9. You, however, are a chosen race, a royal priesthood, a holy nation, a purchased people; that you may proclaim the perfections of him who has called you out of darkness into his marvellous light.   (CCD)

1 John 4:15. Whoever confesses that Jesus is the Son of God, God abides in him, and he in God.   (NASB)

Apocalypse 2:10. Fear none of the things that thou art about to suffer. Behold, the devil is about to cast some of you into prison that you may be tested, and you will have tribulation for ten days. Be thou faithful unto death, and I will give thee the crown of life.   (CCD)

Glossary

Abiogenesis The origin of life from non-living elements, an active field of research among some evolutionary biochemists. Creationists generally reject the results of this research.

Allopolyploidy The state of having two or more sets of chromosomes derived from parents of different species or widely differing strains. If a hybrid is formed between two species, it will usually be sterile because the unlike sets of chromosomes cannot pair normally. If, however, all of the chromosomes are then duplicated, pairing will be possible, and normal fertility will result. Such allopolyploid plants are sterile in crosses to either of the parent species, and hence evolutionary biologists regard them as new species. Creation scientists, however, regard them as hybrids of limited significance.

Analogy Similarity of structure based on similar uses, even though the organisms are unrelated. Wings of birds and bats are analogous.

Angstrom The unit of measure of short wavelength radiation. An Angstrom unit is 1/10,000,000th of a millimeter. 2537 Å is in the ultraviolet range.

Biochemistry The chemistry of the compounds of living organisms and of the processes of life.

Chloroplasts Microscopic bodies within the cytoplasm of plant cells. They contain the green pigment, chlorophyll, which uses solar energy to synthesize carbohydrates from carbon dioxide and water.

Chordate Possessing a dorsal nerve tube; characteristic of the Chordata, a major group of animals including the vertebrates, or animals with backbones.

Chromosome A thread-like body of the cell nucleus, visible under the microscope, especially if stained. Chromosomes consist of DNA complexed with protein. They exist in pairs in the cells of the body, and the number of pairs is characteristic for each species. In sex cells, only one member of each pair of chromosomes is present.

Cladist A biologist whose classification of organisms is based on the principle that splitting of a line of descent into two lines is the most important process of evolution.

Cladogenesis The splitting of a line of descent into two lines; the primary study of a cladist.

Cytochrome c A respiratory enzyme found in all cells, and the subject of some important studies in molecular homology.

Cytology The science of living cells.

DNA Deoxyribonucleic acid, the material in which hereditary information is encoded. It is a major component of chromosomes.

Echinoderm A group of invertebrate animals including sea stars, sea urchins, and their allies. The echinoderm theory proposes that the echinoderms share a common origin with the Chordata.

Endosymbiosis Unlike organisms, with one partner living within the other for their mutual advantage. Thus, blue-green algae may actually live within the cells of other organisms, trading security for the benefits of aerobic respiration.

Genetics The science of heredity and of the control of the processes of life.

Goedel's theorem A theorem by which, in 1931, Goedel demonstrated that any proof of the self-consistency of a logical system would itself include a logical contradiction. This means that there are undecidable propositions. While Goedel's proof applied specifically to mathematical logic, it seems probable that the theorem applies even more rigorously to less exact fields of knowledge. Mathematicians consider Goedel's theorem to be one of the most important results of twentieth-century mathematics.

Hemoglobin The respiratory pigment of red blood cells, composed of a molecule of iron complexed with four protein chains of very specific structure. It also occurs in leguminous plants, where it is called *leghemoglobin*.

Homology Similarity of structure based on details of several systems (skeleton, nerves, blood vessels, muscles, etc.), and hence the antonym of analogy. Creationists attribute this to the common plan of the Creator; ev-

olutionary biologists attribute it to inheritance from a common ancestor.

Ichthyology The scientific study of fishes.

Macroevolution Evolution above the species level, especially as studied in the fossil record. Creation scientists reject this as an untenable hypothesis, while evolutionary biologists consider it a necessary conclusion from their data.

Megaevolution Large-scale evolution, sometimes used as a synonym of macroevolution, and subject to the same differences of evaluation.

Microevolution Change within species, where genetic experimentation may be possible; usually concerned with short time spans.

Miller experiment S. L. Miller mixed water and the gases of the primitive earth. The mixture was sealed into a flask equipped with electrodes, and then heated for a prolonged period. Occasional discharge of sparks simulated lightning. When products were periodically removed from the flask and analyzed, it was found that amino acids and other organic compounds had been synthesized.

Mitochondria Microscopic structures within all cells. They have a specific and complex structure, and they contain the respiratory enzymes. They have been called the powerhouse of the cell.

Monophyly The principle that all members of a species (or a larger unit of classification) are derived from a common ancestor.

Morphology The science of the form and structure of plants and animals.

mRNA Messenger RNA. When genes function, a strand of DNA serves as a template, on which a strand of a closely similar compound, RNA, is synthesized. This then passes from the cell nucleus to the body of the cell, where it functions as a pattern for the synthesis of proteins, most of which serve as enzymes for the control of the processes of life. Because this RNA carries the genetic message from the DNA, it is called messenger RNA, or mRNA.

Mutation   An inheritable change in a gene.

Neo-Darwinism   A union of classical Darwinian selection with modern genetics and other biological sciences. It is currently the dominant theory of evolution and is also called the *synthetic* theory. Creationists regard neo-Darwinism as having no significance beyond certain limits.

Origins model   A scientifically based view concerning the origin of living forms. This term is used extensively by creation scientists, but rarely if ever by evolutionary scientists.

Orthogenesis   A discarded concept of evolution, according to which organisms follow a predetermined course to an inevitable end.

Paleontology   The study of the fossil remains of life of the past.

Phylogenetic series   A series of fossils believed by macroevolutionists to describe the evolutionary history of a species or higher group.

Polymerase   Enzyme that facilitates the formation of polymers. Most biological compounds are made up of many rather similar chemical units that are linked together to form large molecules called polymers. Thus, proteins are polymers of amino acids, DNA of nucleotides, and starches of sugars. DNA polymerase subserves the linkage of many nucleotides to form the complex DNA molecule.

Polyploidy   Duplication of whole sets of chromosomes, so that the nucleus contains more than the usual two sets. See *allopolyploidy* for a particularly important type of polyploidy.

Punctuated equilibrium   A theory, developed especially by Niles Eldredge and Stephen J. Gould, that proposes that species may remain relatively constant (equilibrium) for long periods, and then change rapidly (punctuation).

RNA   *R*ibo*n*ucleic *a*cid. A somewhat simpler nucleic acid than DNA. While DNA carries the genetic information, the several forms of RNA function in the expression of the genetic information.

Scientific creationism   The belief that many evidences in natural science support a rapid formation of distinct kinds by a superior being.

Systematics   The study of the classification of organisms. Partly synonymous with *taxonomy*.

Taxonomy   The system of classification of organisms; the arrangement of plants and animals according to accepted principles.

Transcription   When the DNA molecule serves as a template for the synthesis of the corresponding RNA molecule, one says that the DNA is transcribed into RNA.

Translation   When the mRNA molecule serves as a template for the polymerization of amino acids into a protein molecule, one says that the mRNA molecule is translated to protein.

Suggestions for Further Reading

Bethell, T. February 1985. "Agnostic evolutionists." *Harper's* 270(1617): 49–61.

Clark, H. W. 1968. *Fossils, Flood, and Fire*. Escondido, California: Outdoor Pictures.

Dodson, Edward O. 1984. *The Phenomenon of Man Revisited: A Biological Viewpoint on Teilhard de Chardin*. New York: Columbia University Press.

———— and Peter Dodson. 1985. *Evolution: Process and Product*. 3rd ed. Belmont, California: Wadsworth Publishing Co.

Gish, Duane. 1978. *Evolution: The Fossils Say No!* San Diego, California: Creation-Life Publishers.

Hauret, C. 1964. *Beginnings: Genesis and Modern Science*. Dubuque, Iowa: Priory Press. (Translated from the original French.)

Kerkut, G. A. 1960. *The Implications of Evolution*. New York: Pergamon Press.

Morris, H. M. 1974. *Scientific Creationism*. San Diego, California: Creation-Life Publishers.

Patterson, Colin. 1978. *Evolution*. London and Ithaca, New York: British Museum (Natural History) and Cornell University Press.

Zitterberg, J. P., ed. 1983. *Evolution versus Creationism. The Public Education Controversy*. Phoenix, Arizona: Oryx Press.

Of the above authors, Bethell, Clark, Gish, and Morris are creationists; the Dodsons and Patterson are evolutionary biologists; Hauret is a theologian who tries to show that evolution and Christian faith are not necessarily in conflict; and Kerkut and Zitterberg may be considered neutral, Kerkut because he emphasizes the problems of evolution, Zitterberg because he has assembled essays on both sides of the controversy.